Genealogical Resources within the Jewish Home and Family

Rosemary Wenzerul

Published by
The Federation of Family History Societies (Publications) Ltd
Units 15-16, Chesham Industrial Centre
Oram Street, Bury, Lancashire BL9 6EN

First published 2002

ISBN 1 86006 148 6

Dedicated to the memory of
our dear parents:
Barry and Marjory Molen
Charles and Alice Wenzerul

Printed and bound in the United Kingdom
by the Alden Group, Oxford

CONTENTS

ILLUSTRATIONS

Birth, Death and Marriage Certificates:
Office for National Statistics
© Crown copyright
Reproduced with the permission of the
Controller of Her Majesty's Stationery Office

FOREWORD

'Genealogical Resources within the Jewish Home and Family' is designed to help **ALL members of the family and those who find it difficult to get out and about**. The guide contains copies of the documents and data (which usually go un-noticed), which may be found in most homes. Although some of the information verges on social history, I believe that you can't in fact have one without the other. As the majority of the documents will be found in any home, the guide is not, therefore, pertinent to just the Jewish religion. You may find that your ancestors married into another religion, so some documents appertaining to the Christian religion have also been included.

The information given in this publication is very basic but from such data a tremendous amount of genealogical information may be acquired. Schools may wish to use this guide to teach children genealogy/social history and to make them aware of the importance of keeping such documentation for the benefit of future generations. In addition to show them how to apply the information they gather to expand their family history projects. Perhaps Organisations dealing with the disabled might wish to promote this guide as 'therapy' for disabled people living at home who find it difficult to visit archives and record offices - although nowadays most public places are well equipped for the disabled visitor.

The guide is also intended for people who are unable to go any further backwards in time. Families should be thinking of their descendants and therefore making a start on their current family's records so that in years to come, the information will be well documented.

Because there is so much information in your own home, it may not be necessary when you are first starting genealogy to visit archives and record offices. Once you have acquired all the documentation from within your own family, then it is time to look seriously at the documents you are missing and if you feel they are essential to your research, then it is time to visit the above places.

Being at home, the Internet provides access to a wealth of information. Although the computer is an excellent tool, it is important not to let it become your only interface with the world of genealogy. You will miss out on much of the enjoyment of tracing your family history if you (are unable to) do not also visit libraries, archives, examine original documents, and talk to relatives.

Finally, I would like to thank my husband **Derek Wenzerul** for all his assistance with the technical side of producing the guide because without his continuous help and support with my many computer problems, this publication may not have been completed. In addition, I am extremely grateful to **Alan Simmonds** for the enormous amount of work he has put into our family history and for his continual encouragement, **Caroline Wicks** for writing the sections on Baptism and Confirmation, **Peter Glass** for copies of his family's naturalization papers and **Robert Boyd** for his help and advice on the final layout of the publication. I am indebted to my dear parents and aunt, the **late Barry and Marjory Molen (nee Goldston)** and **Betty Molen** who had saved so many documents over the years and to the **Barnett, Baskin, Benjamin, Bluestone, Davis, Feldman, Goldston, Greenman, Holness, Jacobus, Molen/Vandermolen, Myers and Wenzerul families** for allowing me access to their personal documentation and photographs.

Rosemary Wenzerul *January 2002*

INTRODUCTION

Have you ever wondered how your grandparents and great grandparents lived? What their homes were like, what food they ate, did they struggle to survive with so many children to feed and what life was generally like when they were alive? (There are books available on social history, which do give descriptions of the life in the 18th and 19th century.) This unfortunately a number of people will never know, as they have left it too late to ask their relatives, so it is important to start your family history while you are still young. You are under no pressure where genealogy is concerned. You can begin your research at any age (as I have said above, the younger the better), leave it for a time and then resume again in years to come.

In the 20th century, I think you will agree that the world achieved more in the way of science and technology than in any other century. So many inventions and improvements have taken place during this period. When I was a child, people used to talk about 'the man in the moon' but I never thought the day would come when men actually landed on the moon.

Well, back down to earth. We are now in the 21st century with so much technology on offer to us. The Internet has a wealth of information and access to so many public records is now possible.

Because we are limited as to how far back we can go into our ancestors past, it is so important to concentrate on helping future generations.

The Bible emphasizes the fact that it is everyone's duty to pass on information from generation to generation.

Remember the days of old, consider the years of many generations:
Ask thy father, and he will declare unto thee: Thine elders, and they
will tell thee.

Deuteronomy XXX11 v.7

The idea of this guide is to take you on a journey from the cradle to the grave. To show you how easy it is to gather information along the way from existing records you may have in your home and that you don't have to spend hours of your time in libraries, record offices or archives. Our intention is that you will find some ideas out of the many given and work on these.

I should mention that most of the dates, names and addresses, which appear in the documents within this guide, are fictitious.

Addresses of all Organisations mentioned throughout the guide plus others are listed at the back. If you are unable to visit these places, then it is just as easy to write to them direct.

Good luck with your research.

Rosemary Wenzerul

WHERE DO I BEGIN?

It is important to interview as many relatives as possible, preferably starting with the eldest. The following is an example of a very short dialogue between a fictitious mother and her daughter. From this example you will notice how much information may be obtained by keeping your interview short and to the point and that you don't have to spend hours recording your interview and transcribing it to obtain all of the facts. **Use this example to help obtain information from your own family.** Reference to this story will be given throughout this guide. To help you, I have numbered the text and have shown below how to use/find the information you have obtained from this interview.

My mother, your grandmother Miriam - her single name was Barnett, was born on [1]31 November 1888 and lived at [2]121 Artillery Passage, in the East End of London. She had 4 sisters and 3 brothers, but she was the youngest as far as I know. I think she went to the [3]Jews' Free School but I am not sure. However, I do know that your grandfather went to Kings College, London. Perhaps you could write to the College and ask for details. Well going back to your Grandmother. She was on her way to work one day and bumped into an old friend called David Israel and on the [4]30 February 1911, 18 months after they had once again met, they married. The wedding was held at the [5]Bevis Marks Synagogue. They lived in the East End for about 10 years but as David's family all lived in Brighton, they moved there around 1921 - you would have to ask [6]Papa for the name of the road and if he remembers the date.

Uncle Jonathan (who was my brother) was killed during the First World War. He joined the First Surrey Rifles and was killed in France aged 19 on the 31 September 1917. Unfortunately, I don't think any of the family knows where he is [7]buried.

My sister Agnes, who [8]died on the 31 April 1954, you remember Aunty Agnes, she had a wonderful [9]recipe for stuffed monkey - she also won the national award for flower arranging in 1949 - her photo appeared in the [10]Daily Sketch newspaper receiving the medal. She also left the family a lot of money in her [11]will. I just remembered that your great grandfather was made a [12]Freeman of the City of London in 1856 and I have the certificate which I will give to you. Uncle Jack might help you as he belonged to a family history society and I think he may have started a [13]family tree so do contact him before you begin your research. This is all I can remember for the time being, I hope it has been of help.

References:

1 Obtain a copy of the birth certificate, if not available from your family, one may be obtained from Family Record Centre (FRC) or Public Record Office (PRO) (addresses on page 99). Ask the family if any photos are available of him/her as a baby.

2 Visit the FRC or PRO and look at the 1891 Census and at the Electoral Registers. You may find more children than your mother remembered. Ask what living in those days was like and what sort of house they lived in. See if the property still exists, if so, visit and take a photograph.

3 The (LMA) London Metropolitan Archives (address on page 99) has the admission registers of the (JFS) Jews' Free School and other schools.

4 Obtain a copy of the marriage certificate, if the family haven't got a copy, one may be obtained from the FRC or PRO. Ask the family for photos of the wedding, memorabilia and a copy of the Ketubah (Marriage Contract).

5 Bevis Marks Synagogue have published many of their records of births, marriages, deaths and circumcisions (see pages 79 and 101).

6 Ensure you find out 'papa's' correct name. Is your mother referring to your grandfather or to your father? Always check on any family nicknames.

7 Contact the Commonwealth War Grave Commission (web-site: see page 103) to find out where he was buried. Excellent information is given about each serviceman. Ask the family if they have a photo of him in uniform or as a civilian. If you are going abroad do visit the cemetery and photograph the grave. Find out rank and service number, letters sent to loved ones, stories about the war.

8 Obtain a copy of the death certificate from a member of the family, if not available, one may be obtained from the FRC or PRO (addresses on page 99). Ask which cemetery she is buried in and visit the grave - take a photo of the grave and make a note of the grave location reference number for your records.

9 Ask if the recipe still exists, if so make a note of it for future generations to enjoy. Ensure you say whose recipe it was. If it was very decorative, take a photograph.

10 Visit the British Library Newspaper Library (address on page 100) and look at the Daily Sketch newspapers for this particular period.

11 Visit the FRC or PRO and look at probate and wills.

12 Details concerning Freemen of the City of London and copies of the certificates may be obtained from the Corporation of London Record Office, Guildhall (address on page 100). Example on page 14 is a copy of the certificate.

13 Before you start any research, always ask if there is a copy of the family tree available. This will save you a lot of unnecessary work if it has already been started by one of your relatives.

From this very short story you can identify the relationships within your family. A vast amount of valuable information may be obtained from documents, photographs and memorabilia seen whilst interviewing relatives. Where possible copies should be made of this information, and of course, documents obtained from the various Resource Centres. All this information should be placed in your family history file.

Remember, every person has a story to tell, whether it be of their earliest memories, school days, achievements, career, hobbies, engagement, marriage, honeymoon, divorce, family or friends. They may have served overseas in the forces and can tell you some of their experiences. There is therefore so much information just sitting in your family waiting for you to find out and record for future generations to enjoy and cherish. Make the most of the information you have gained and make a start on your family history now.

Freeman of the City of London Certificate

 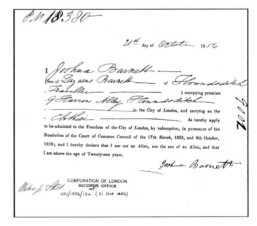

Note that the person declares that he is not an alien, nor the son of an alien, and that he is above the age of twenty-one years. Therefore he was born in this country and so was his father. It also shows the name of his father and his address in 1856.

14

WHAT SHOULD I DO WITH THE INFORMATION COLLECTED?

As previously stated the information from the interview will be referred to throughout the guide, so that each section covered will refer back to the interview. It is important to observe how one small piece of information can lead to gathering an enormous amount of data. There are numerous documents, however, which are not mentioned in the interview but examples of which are shown in the guide and will be of additional help to you.

FOLDERS

Before you start collecting any data I suggest you purchase a couple of large ring binder files with dividers and use each section for a different part of your family. Ensure you label your ring binders accordingly. Suggested sections could be births, marriages, deaths, property, family at war, schooldays, games, employment etc.

PRESERVATION OF DOCUMENTS

Preservation of documents is very important, so ensure you store your data in suitable sleeves or files. If you decide to use plastic folders, make sure they are the ones that will not lift off the print.

BREAKING DOWN YOUR DATA

If you have a large family and have collected a lot of information, it will be easier to break the family down into appropriate family sections. For instance, if your grandparents had 8 children, then each section of your folder should be split into 8 sections to allow the data collected from these children's families to be included and to follow through their individual lives and those of their children.

EXISTING FAMILY TREES

The story mentioned that uncle Jack might have started a family tree, so before you do anything, do check whether any relation has produced a family tree - this will save you a lot of work if they have.

Let us imagine that your uncle does have a tree. It may well be a handwritten one, very old, fragile and impossible to add any more information to. With today's technology and a selection of very easy family history computer programmes which are available on the market it is very easy to take the data from the handwritten sheet and produce a computerised family tree.

Computerised programmes are very flexible and so much easier to up-date. On the next page are examples of the various formats you can use. Both these examples are correct; it is just a matter of preference as to which one you decide to use.

In addition, you may wish to enhance your family tree by adding photographs as the example below shows.

```
              #113
           Harry Myers
   9 May 1883 - 7 Jul 1953
         m. ??  ___  1904
         Kate Barnett
   29 Jul 1883 - 9 Jul 1946
```

TREE CHART

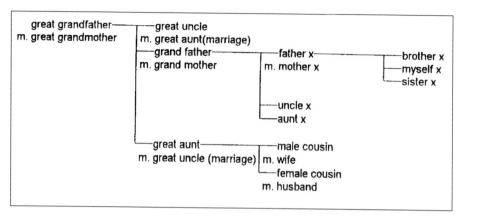

BOX CHART

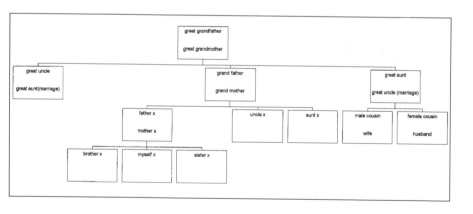

RE-PHOTOGRAPHING OLD PHOTOGRAPHS
AND DOCUMENTS

You may find that your relatives have old photo albums and the photos may be so old and fragile that you don't want to touch them and the negatives are long gone - well you don't need to spend a lot of money having them copied professionally. It is so easy to re-photograph them in situ at home. It is preferable to use a reflex camera (where the viewfinder actually looks through the camera lens) fitted with a close-focusing lens. If you decide to do this yourself, it is cheaper to use colour film and process it locally rather than purchasing black and white film unless you print it yourself. In addition, one should index both old and new negatives and store them in a cool, dry, dark place. If you have a computer with a flatbed scanner, you can also copy larger photos using that.

When looking at old photographs, notice the fashion of the day - sometimes dating old photos may be ascertained from the clothes worn.

FAMILY HISTORY SOCIETIES (FHS)

The Federation of Family History Societies (FFHS) was founded in 1974 and has branches all over the UK and abroad. It has many publications and publishes the Family History News and Digest twice a year. Even if you are at home, it is well worth joining your local FHS. To find out the address, contact your local reference library. Most Societies hold regular meetings and lectures, produce their own journals or newsletters and can be a tremendous help to a beginner.

The Jewish Genealogical Society of Great Britain (JGSGB) holds most of its meetings in N.W. London. They have a journal and newsletter, regular monthly meetings, special interest groups (Latvia, Lithuania, Holland, Anglo-Jewish, Germany, Poland and Galicia), regional groups, family history workshops, library, one to one mentoring and lots more. (JGSGB address is on page 101).

HOW TO ENLARGE MY FAMILY HISTORY?

Although going back so many generations is a great achievement, it can also be rather boring just looking at pages and pages of names and dates without any further information to back up your data.

We will continue by identifying the various documents you may collect during your lifetime:

BIRTH CERTIFICATE

According to the story, my mother told me that my Grandmother Miriam, was born on the 31 November 1888 and lived at 121 Artillery Passage in the East End of London. Luckily, Uncle Jack had a copy of her birth certificate. The copies of the remaining children's birth certificates may be obtained from the Family Record Centre or Public Record Office (addresses on page 99) at the current cost of £6.50 per certificate - but check with other members of the family first to see if they have copies:

A birth certificate is not just a piece of paper to keep safely in the drawer. Have a look at the enormous amount of information a full certificate contains (copy on page 22) **The date and place of birth, name, sex, father's name, mother's name (including maiden name), father's occupation, the address of the informant and the date registered**.

Keep it safely but do take an A4 photocopy and file it in alphabetical order in your family history file under the 'birth section' and include the details in your family tree so in years to come, future generations will have a true record of your birth. You may find that the family only has a **short birth certificate,**

missing a lot of details (as shown below) - it is always possible to obtain the full information from the previously mentioned organisations.

BIRTHS AND DEATHS REGISTRATION ACT, 1874.

CERTIFICATE of REGISTRY of BIRTH.

I, the undersigned, Do hereby certify that the Birth of Cyril Baron Benjamin *born on the* 11th *day of* May 19 06, *has been duly registered by me at Entry No.* 156 *of my Register Book No.* 48

Witness *my hand, this* 21st *day of* June 19 06

Walter Davison } Registrar of *Births and Deaths.*

West Ham *District.* Forest Gale *Sub-District.*
[OVER.

Birmingham: Printed by Authority of the Registrar-General by Martin Billing, Son, and Co., Livery Street,

Birth Certificate

CERTIFIED COPY OF AN ENTRY OF BIRTH

GIVEN AT THE GENERAL REGISTER OFFICE

Application Number ......Woo7630l......

REGISTRATION DISTRICT ...... Mile End Old Town ......

1881. BIRTH in the Sub-district of ...Mile End Old Town Western... in the County of ...Middlesex...

Columns:-	1	2	3	4	5	6	7	8	9	10*
No.	When and where born	Name, if any	Sex	Name and surname of father	Name, surname and maiden surname of mother	Occupation of father	Signature, description and residence of informant	When registered	Signature of registrar	Name entered after registration
153	Seventieth March 1881 56 New Road	David	Boy	Jacob Van der Molen	Elizabeth Van der Molen formerly de Vries	Barber	J Van der Molen father 56 New Road Mile End.	Twenty-third April 1881.	John B. Ratcliff Registrar	

CERTIFIED to be a true copy of an entry in the certified copy of a Register of Births in the District above mentioned

Given at the GENERAL REGISTER OFFICE, under the Seal of the said Office, the ...19th... day of ...February... 19 98.

*See note overleaf

BXBY 353494

CAUTION:- It is an offence to falsify a certificate or to make or knowingly use a false certificate or a copy of a false certificate intending it to be accepted as genuine to the prejudice of any person or to possess a certificate knowing it to be false without lawful authority.

WARNING: THIS CERTIFICATE IS NOT EVIDENCE OF THE IDENTITY OF THE PERSON PRESENTING IT.

Dd 0034 200M 12/97 Mcr(202471)

BAPTISM

You may discover amongst your ancestor's papers that a member of the family married a non-Jewish person at some time in the past. Therefore, descendants of that person may have brought their children up as Christians. The children may have been Baptised and Confirmed in Church.

In the Anglican Church Baptism of infants is usual, although Baptism of older children and adults is not unknown. The certificate of Baptism below shows: **the child's name and his sponsors who would be his godparents plus the date and the name of the church**.

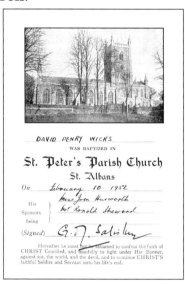

David Penry Wicks
WAS BAPTIZED IN
St. Peter's Parish Church
St. Albans
On *February 10. 1952*
His Sponsors being *Marie John Husworth*
Mr. Ronald Sheward
(Signed) *G.D.J. Salisbury*
Hereafter he must not be ashamed to confess the faith of CHRIST Crucified, and manfully to fight under His Banner, against sin, the world, and the devil, and to continue CHRIST'S faithful Soldier and Servant unto his life's end.

BIRTH AND BABY RELATED MEMORABILIA

If your parents or family have baby photos ask for copies and include them in your file. Ensure you write/type the name of the baby and date taken on reverse or underneath the photo and whose baby it is. Special pens, which will not damage your photos, may be purchased from camera shops or stationers.

Have your own, or your family's, children's birth announcement been entered in the newspapers such as the Jewish Chronicle? Do look at these carefully - these small entries show: names of parents, where the baby was born, date of birth, name of the other siblings, names of both grandparents and great-grandparents. Make a note of which edition of the newspaper it came from and include all these details in your family history.

> **COHEN/LEVY** Janice and Sidney are delighted to announce the safe arrival of JENNIFER ANN in Jerusalem on 30 February 1911. Sister for Daniel and Peter, Sixth grandchild for Annie and Jeffrey Cohen and Sadie and Alfred Levy, third great-grandchild for Marjory Levy.

(Fictitious information given)

Keep your baby's first lock of hair and other baby bits and pieces. Include a photograph of your children at kindergarten. Make a note of your baby's early words and their meaning also record any family sayings. I don't know about your family, but our family had numerous sayings and words, some very descriptive ones.

CIRCUMCISION (B'rit Milah)

B'rit Milah: This is the ceremony of circumcision, whereby every Jewish male child is initiated into the Covenant of Abraham (Lev. 12, 3) on the eighth day after birth. If for medical reasons it cannot be carried out on the eighth day then the circumcision may be delayed.

Your new baby son has been circumcised, the Mohel (Person qualified to carry out the procedure) may give you a certificate similar to the one shown on the next page (South African example): The information given is: **Father's name, whether Jewish by birth or converted, if converted, state place, date and by whom, whether you are the natural or adopted child of your parents**.

Mother's name and maiden name, whether Jewish by birth or converted, if converted, state place, date and by whom, whether you are the natural or adopted child of your parents.

General information - address, telephone number, date of marriage of parents and where solemnised, English name of child, Hebrew name of Father, is Father Cohen, Levi or Yisroel (see glossary on page 105), date and approximate time of birth, proposed date of B'rit Milah, actual date of B'rit Milah, space for remarks and the signature of the Mohel and the parents.

Although I have erased all the information from the form on the next page, the original document showed the full name, address and telephone number of the Mohel.

Union of Orthodox Synagogues of South Africa

(Incorporated Association not for gain)
Formerly Federation of Synagogues of South Africa

Form of Registration for Brit Mila
(Ritual Circumcision)

A 82

Date: ....

A. FATHER:

1. Name: ....

2. State whether Jewish by birth, or converted: ....

3. If converted, state place, date and by whom: ....

4. Are you the natural or adopted child of your parents? ....

B. MOTHER:

1. Name and maiden name: ....

2. State whether Jewish by birth, or converted: ....

3. If converted, state place, date and by whom: ....

4. Are you the natural or adopted child of your parents? ....

C. GENERAL INFORMATION:

1. Address: .... Phones (Res.) ....

    .... (Bus.) ....

    ....

2. Date of marriage of parents and where solemnised: ....

    ....

3. English name of child: ....

4. Hebrew name of child: ....

5. Hebrew name of Father: ....

6. Is Father Cohen, Levi or Yisroel: ....

D. 1. Date and approximate time of birth: ....

2. Proposed date of Brit Mila: ....

3. Actual date of Brit Mila: ....

REMARKS

....

....

Signature of Mohel: ....   Signature of Parent: ....

26

FAMILY BIBLES

If you have inherited a family bible continue to keep the information up to date and pass it on to future generations.

Family bibles are very personal things and show how each generation took the trouble of carefully recording the births, marriages and deaths of their family. **The example below shows the English and Hebrew dates plus the Hebrew names of the people listed.**

The first entry in this bible is 1873

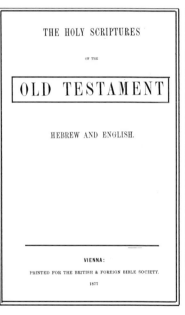

SCHOOLDAYS

Mention in the story was made of the JFS (Jews' Free School). The old admission registers for this school and others are on microfilm and are now held by the London Metropolitan Archives (address on page 99). **The following example shows extracts from the school admission books for Stepney Jewish School and Rutland Street Infant School. The information gives the name of the student, address, date of birth and admission date. In some cases if he came from/went to another school**. Once you have collected all the information you have at home and from your family, then if you felt it necessary, it would be a good idea to visit the archives and look at the admission books.

```
┌─────────────────────────────────────────────────────────────────────┐
│  EXTRACTS FROM SCHOOL ADMISSIONS BOOKS                               │
│                                                                       │
│  No. ─────────────────────  Parent/guardian ────────────            │
├─────────────────────────────────────────────────────────────────────┤
│  STEPNEY JEWISH SCHOOL      [X95/23]                                 │
│  430   John De Fries        135  Skidmore  St.    Adm  24/9/83  (no  │
│                             d.o.b.)                                   │
│  1019 Barnett Defries       7 Leslie  Street  b. -/3/83. Adm. ?2/90  │
│                             from Inf Dept. Left 12/3/97.             │
│  1483 Harry Defries         10 Leslie  St   b. -/11/86   Adm. 7/2/94 │
│                             from Infants Dept.  Left 10/12/94        │
│  1554 David Defries         87  Skidmore  St    b.  10/9/86.    Adm. │
│                             13/8/94 from Trafalgar St.               │
├─────────────────────────────────────────────────────────────────────┤
│  RUTLAND STREET INFANTS 1899-1910   EO/DIV 5/RUT/A&D/2               │
│                                                                       │
│  68    Louis Molen          s/o  Henry. 257 Commercial Road.  b. 13  │
│                             Mar 1894. Admitted  3/7/99 from Dempsey  │
│                             Street.  ??Left 29/6/99                  │
├─────────────────────────────────────────────────────────────────────┤
│  RUTLAND STREET INFANTS 1885-1890 EO/DIV 5/RUT/A&D/1                 │
│                                                                       │
│  1428 Esther Defries        d/o Henry & Ada.  76 Sidney St.   b. 23  │
│                             Jan 1885. Adm. 29/4/89 "Readmitted"      │
│  1429 David Defries         s/o Henry & Ada.  76 Sidney St.  b. 12   │
│                             Sep 1886                                  │
│  839   David Vandermolen    s/o  Jacob & Betsy. 56 New Road.  b. 16  │
│                             Mar  1881.  Adm.  22/8/87 from  Settles  │
│                             Street.  Left  17/10/87 "Gone  to  Boys  │
│                             School"                                   │
│  840   Isaac Vandermolen    s/o  Jacob & Betsy. 56 New Road.  b. 28  │
│                             Sep 1883.  Adm 22/8/87.  No prev. school │
└─────────────────────────────────────────────────────────────────────┘
```

Whatever school you attended, keep photos of yourself taken at school each year and notice how you change with age. Include the date of the photograph, the name of the person and the name of the school on the reverse. Do the same for group photographs as well.

Are you about to go to a new school? Are you excited or a bit nervous? What was your first day like? Do write a few lines on how you feel and the names of your friends who will be going with you. How much did your school uniform cost? Today, you certainly can't buy the complete uniform for the equivalent of the amount shown on the price list below.

The uniform price list below dates from 1957-8.

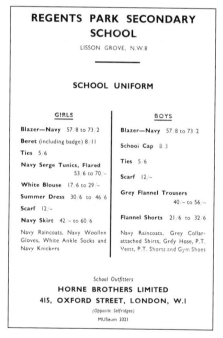

REGENTS PARK SECONDARY SCHOOL

LISSON GROVE, N.W.8

SCHOOL UNIFORM

GIRLS	BOYS
Blazer—Navy 57/8 to 73/2	Blazer—Navy 57/8 to 73/2
Beret (including badge) 8/11	School Cap 8/3
Ties 5/6	
Navy Serge Tunics, Flared 53/6 to 70/-	Ties 5/6
	Scarf 12/-
White Blouse 17/6 to 29/-	
Summer Dress 30/6 to 46/6	Grey Flannel Trousers 40/- to 56/-
Scarf 12/-	
Navy Skirt 42/- to 60/6	Flannel Shorts 21/6 to 32/6
Navy Raincoats, Navy Woollen Gloves, White Ankle Socks and Navy Knickers	Navy Raincoats, Grey Collar-attached Shirts, Grey Hose, P.T. Vests, P.T. Shorts and Gym Shoes

School Outfitters
HORNE BROTHERS LIMITED
415, OXFORD STREET, LONDON, W.I
(Opposite Selfridges)
MUSeum 3321

SCHOOL REPORTS

How did you do at school? Your school reports will indicate this. Details shown will be: **the name of the school, the years you attended and will be signed by your form teacher or head teacher.**

CERTIFICATES/AWARDS

Did you learn to swim at school or win an end of term prize? (See page 34). If so, take photocopies of the diplomas. Perhaps your prize was a book - note the inscription. Write a couple of lines next to them saying how you won them.

TOYS AND GAMES

Keep a record of the toys you had at home and the games you played at school, for example, leap frog, hopscotch, marbles, jacks, conkers, five stones, skipping and note the rules of the games. I read that skipping, conkers and British bulldog may be banned from certain school playgrounds as they are thought to be too dangerous! Therefore keep a note of the rhymes you put to various games, as in years to come, games such as skipping, may become a game of the past - for example (I'm a girl guide dressed in blue, these are the actions I must do. Salute to the Queen, bow to the King, turn right round and count 16.)

Don't forget the games you played at home - snakes and ladders, ludo, scrabble, monopoly because in years to come board games may no longer exist as computer games may become the games of the future. If you don't want to keep the games, take photocopies of the board and the rules of the game and file them in your folder.

BUS TICKETS

How did you travel to school? Perhaps you still have some bus tickets from when you were a child. **These will show the price of the ticket at the time and the bus route taken. The hole in the ticket indicates the destination/fare point.**

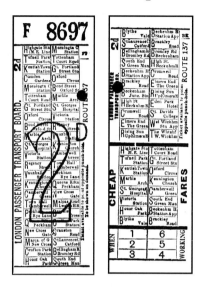

CHILDHOOD MEMORIES

Take time every so often to write down your childhood memories. **For example, on your way to school, do you remember the sweet shop you visited? My memories are as follow:**

The shop was tiny and was crowded with other children, it had a very small counter sandwiched between two scruffy glass cabinets displaying chocolates and cigarettes (Craven A, Woodbines, Players) and when the season was right the cabinets displayed fireworks.

The old wooden shelves at the back of the shop supported ranks of heavy, screw-topped glass sweet jars. I can still hear the ping of aniseed balls dropping into the copper scales and the crack of the metal hammer breaking the toffee or smashing the cough candy.

Beside the scales was the till, a simple wooden drawer with compartments for coins, notes and in those days of rationing, sweet coupons. In my childhood you could buy sweets for as little as a farthing? You could buy 4 chews for an old penny; flying saucers were 2 a penny. The sweet shop assistant would weigh the sweets and then put them into a brown paper bag. Those were the days.

Therefore, make a note of the confectionary you liked eating as a child and of course the sweets you enjoy today. Keep the sweet wrappers - they are very colourful (if you don't eat sweets, ask children to save the wrappers for you). So many sweets are no longer available, for instance - tiger nuts, palm toffee, brandy balls, bootlaces, clove balls and many more.

The crisp wrapper below shows **the year of promotion - 'Awards for Schools 1999'** and the sweet packet indicates the **sell by date** and **how much the product costs**. Keeping these packets will indicate to future generations when the merchandise was available and they will be able to compare future prices.

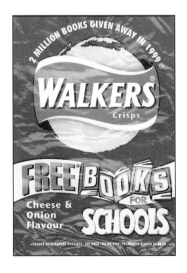

COMICS AND MAGAZINES

Remember to include details of the comics and magazines you read as a child, maybe you still have copies. During the Second World War the comics available were Knockout, Triumph, Wizard, etc. In the 1950's you had Beezer, Eagle, Girl, School Friend, Tiger, Topper - all of these are no longer available. If you take time to note the ones you enjoy reading today, children in the future will be pleased to have this information.

POPULAR MUSIC

In the 1950's was the arrival of Rock 'n' roll - do you remember Bill Haley and the Comets, Elvis Presley with his Heartbreak Hotel and Blue Suede Shoes? On television there was 'Take your Pick' with Michael Miles and many more well known artists - Adam Faith, Cliff Richard and Tommy Steele to name but a few. These were wonderful years for the teenager as too are today's groups - Boyzone, S Club 7, the Spice Girls and many more. Whatever era you lived through you will have fond memories of your time at dances, discos etc so write about your teenage years. Were you at school when you were mad about Elvis Presley, did you see him live? Do you have his autograph? There are all sorts of things you can write about that will be of interest in years to come.

TEENAGE FASHION

Did you live through the 'mini', or the 'maxi' period? Were you a goth, skinhead, or a teddy boy? Did you have long or short hair? Perhaps you had a mohican hair cut died bright orange! Did you wear winkle pickers or platform shoes? The fashion each year or decade will change, as you will see from history books. Therefore, in 50 or 100 years from now, the clothing and hairstyles you have at the moment will be in the history books too! So as I have said throughout this guide, write about yourself.

SPORTS

What events did you take part in? Did you gain a certificate for swimming? Perhaps you broke the school record for long jump. Maybe the football team you played with became top of the league. All these achievements and issues come into your family history and should be recorded.

BAR-MITZVAH/BAT-MITZVAH

Bar-Mitzvah: Son of the Commandments. Following a boy's 13th birthday, he is called up in the synagogue to read a portion of the Law. At the age of 13 he reaches his religious majority and Jewish law recognises his responsibility under the Law from then onwards.

You are now a young man or woman. Include photographs of your Bar-Mitzvah or Bat-Mitzvah in your family history file - remember to date them.

Keep your certificate and gift received from the Synagogue in a safe place. The following are the inscriptions on the inside covers of a Siddur (see glossary on page 105) presented to a father and son. Note: **Name and address of Synagogue, name of recipient, names of the Ministers and the English and Hebrew date.**

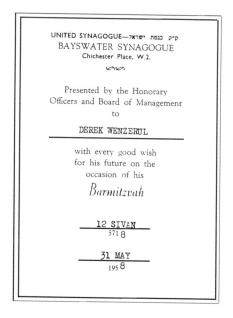

Teesdale Street Talmud Torah

Presented to :-

Master Charles
Wenzerul

on the occasion of
his Barmitzvah.
3rd November 1928

Chairman : P. Ackerman Esq,
Vice Chairman: S. Pescoviteh Esq.
Treasurer : S. Levin Esq.
Secretary : A. Bussin Esq.
Trustee : A. Plaskow Esq.
Headmaster

UNITED SYNAGOGUE—ק"ק כנסת ישראל
BAYSWATER SYNAGOGUE
Chichester Place, W.2.

Presented by the Honorary
Officers and Board of Management
to

DEREK WENZERUL

with every good wish
for his future on the
occasion of his

Barmitzvah

12 SIVAN
5718

31 MAY
1958

Bat-Mitzvah: Girls are usually aged 12 when they have their Bat-Mitzvah. Example of the certificate below:

INVITATIONS

Retain a copy of the invitation and note the details. The invitation below shows: **the names of the parents, their son (they obviously have other children as the invitation says 'youngest'), synagogue name and address, date of Bar-Mitzvah, the date and place of the reception plus their home address.**

Andrea & Simon Levy
request the pleasure of the company of

_____

to celebrate the Bar-Mitzvah of their youngest son
David Michael
who will read Sidrah, Maftir & Haftarah
at the New West End Synagogue,
St. Petersburgh Place, London, W.2.
on Saturday, 30 February 1973

Kiddush after the Service in the Synagogue Hall
Dinner & Ball on Sunday, 31 February 1973
at the Royal Majestic Suite, Willesden Lane, N.W.6

R.S.V.P.
1496 Gordon Avenue
Bayswater, London, W.2.

Reception 5 pm
Dinner 6 pm

(Fictitious information given)

Make a note of your **Hebrew Name, the portion read** (see below), the names of your family who were called-up to the Reading of the Torah (see glossary on page 105).

> Baruch ben Dovid
> Korach (Numbers)
> Maftir & Haftarah Korach
> (I Samuel XI 14 - XII 22)

(Fictitious information given)

Record the names of your family and friends who were invited - keep copies of the table plan, memorabilia eg matchboxes, yarmulka, menu etc (they nearly always have names and dates printed on them) or just a list of your friends and family who were sent invitations.

CONFIRMATION

As I have mentioned under the Baptism section, you may discover amongst your ancestor's papers that a member of the family married a non-Jewish person at some time in the past. Therefore, descendants of that person may have brought their children up as Christians. The children may have been confirmed and Baptised in Church.

Confirmation in the Anglican Church usually takes place between the ages of 10-15 but it can be younger. Confirmation is the time when the person takes for themselves the promises which were made on their behalf at Baptism (by parents or Godparents) and it is a statement of faith or a public demonstration of faith - a time when the person stands up before the Bishop and then kneels to receive a blessing and confirmation of G-d's life in theirs. Participation in communion (bread and wine) follows confirmation although there is currently a debate about whether Christian children should be admitted to communion before confirmation.

Opposite is a copy of a certificate of confirmation showing **the persons name, date of confirmation and the name of the Church**.

Diocese of Saint Albans

David Nicks was confirmed on *30th April 1980* at *St. Albans Abbey*

UNIVERSITY/COLLEGE

According to the story, knowing that my grandfather had gone to Kings College, I wrote to them. I received a reply, which confirmed the courses he had taken in order to qualify and his years of attendance. Therefore, it is well worth writing to schools, colleges or universities to ask if they hold records.

As I mentioned earlier most school records may be found at the London Metropolitan Archives (address on page 99) including those of the JFS - Jews' Free School.

GRADUATION CEREMONY

Whatever University or College you go to your big day will come - your graduation ceremony.

Keep photos of your graduation in your family history file. In addition, note the date of the ceremony and the name of the university. Also keep copies of your certificates gained throughout your school/college life.

DETAILS OF THE DAY

Take time and write a few lines about the events of the day. Who officiated at the ceremony, the friends who also graduated, the excitement of your family etc.

PITMANS COLLEGE

SOUTHAMPTON ROW
LONDON · W·C·1

AND BRANCHES

ROSEMARY   E.   MOLEN

HAVING FOLLOWED A SUITABLE COURSE OF STUDY AND HAVING UNDERGONE THE EXAMINATION PRESCRIBED BY THE COLLEGE HAS BEEN AWARDED THIS CERTIFICATE FOR

PITMAN'S SHORTHAND THEORY

I. j. Pitman. *CPitman*

Roh. H. Holland *M.V Graham.*

41

HOBBIES AND INTERESTS

Did your ancestors have a favourite hobby? In the story Aunt Agnes won the national award for flower arranging in 1949 and a photo of herself receiving her medal was in the Daily Sketch Newspaper. If the family haven't got copies of the newspaper concerned, visit the British Library Newspaper Library in Colindale (address on page 100) and obtain a photocopy.

Perhaps a member of your family enjoyed gardening, specialising in certain flowers and entered them for horticultural shows. Did they win a cup or certificate? If they did, keep the certificates in a safe place, or perhaps a shield for the best in show - take a photo of them holding the shield.

Silver Jubilee Shield - Harrow Show 1985
Awarded for highest points in all
Painting Classes

Charles of London Cup
Harrow Show - 1986
Awarded for highest points in Arts & Crafts

Have their names appeared in the newspapers? Obtain copies of the newspapers from the Newspaper Library shown above. Maybe they loved painting or making models and organised an exhibition of their work. Perhaps there was a brochure given out at the exhibition with his/her name in it. All this information is invaluable.

YOUTH ORGANISATIONS

Were you a member of the scouts or guides or other youth organisation? If so, keep a photo of yourself in uniform and any certificates you may have gained. Tell stories of the funny experiences you may have had in one of these organisations. If you were a St. John's Ambulance Cadet for instance, name the locations where you were on duty - for example, it could have been in a theatre, cinema, ice-rink or football match.

HOLIDAYS

Write about your holidays as a child and if you returned to the same place as an adult - were you disappointed to find it had changed?

Take photos of the family on the beach and notice how the fashion has changed. If you know their names, where the photo was taken and the year, make a note of this. Looking at the photo below, just think how 'free' we are today just wearing swimsuits or bikinis as opposed to being fully dressed in such uncomfortable clothing. Photograph your children. Perhaps you enjoyed a relaxing fishing trip in the Lake District. All of these photographs will help enhance your family history and will illustrate any stories you have.

Yarmouth Sands. July 26th 1909.

PASSENGER LIST

Your ancestors cruised to the U.S.A. and you have come across the passenger list with their name included. Why did they go? How long did the cruise take? What sort of send off did they have from Southampton or wherever the ship sailed from? All these questions can make up a story against this document.

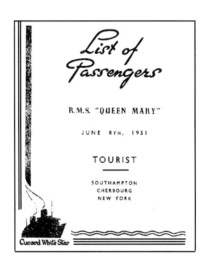

PASSPORTS

Look at passports as these have a lot of personal information about the person. The example on the following page shows: **profession, place and date of birth, where he lived, his height, colour of eyes and colour of hair. In addition, you also have a photograph and signature and the Foreign Office date stamp. You may find that old passports have been date stamped showing the various countries visited.**

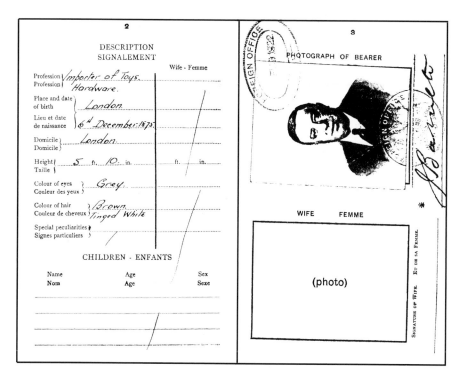

FAMILY RECIPES

My mother in the story mentioned that Aunt Agnes had a wonderful recipe for stuffed monkey. Most families have recipes, which have been handed down from generation to generation. It is so important for these to continue through future generations - so make the effort and write them out. If the finished recipe looks very appetising, take a photo of it. **Remember to record the origin and the name of the person who gave it. If you have a photograph of the person, include this too**.

THEN AND NOW

PEOPLE

Keep photographs commemorating various stages of your life. Perhaps your family have a group photograph of themselves as children and another when they were adults as the photographs below illustrate.

BUILDINGS

If you have photos of where your family lived or worked, go back and see if the buildings are still there. If they are, take photographs and record the date taken.

If the property was in the East End of London or places like Coventry then due to the bombing in the War and the redevelopment of the area, it is unlikely that the building still survives. However, having said this, there are still a number of properties that are still standing. Have a look at old maps of the area.

You will notice the example below shows that the Baker shop has changed into a Tyre shop. **However if you look carefully at the building of the tyre shop, you will notice that the window over the door and the window and door at the side are now missing.** The photo of the building was taken roughly 80 years later.

MEMORABILIA

It is important to keep memorabilia or family treasures. If you ask your relatives to show you any memorabilia they have, you will be surprised what they come up with. **In fact, looking through old keepsakes jogs the memory and all sorts of stories may emerge. Do try and record any stories your relatives may have, or ask them to write them down for you.**

Start a collection of out of date plastic cards, these will give future generations an idea of your interests. Or if you had a collection of old postcards, these will bring back memories of the holidays you once had.

Objects with inscriptions - **ask about the history surrounding these.**

DANCE CARDS

In the years gone by it was the custom when one attended a tea dance to have a dance card and against each dance one would name the person you intended to dance with. **If you find one of these, perhaps you can recognise some of the names.**

DANCES		ENGAGEMENTS
1. Valse ... ..."Santiago"	1.	Mrs Def...
2. Lancers "My Lady Molly"	2.	Mrs Benjamin
3. Valse ... " Blue Danube"	3.	
4. Alberts ... " Mikado"	4.	Mrs Bismarck
5. Barn Dance ... " Coo-ce"	5.	Mrs Def...
6. Valse ... " Salut D Amour"	6.	
7. Lancers ... " Three Little Maids"	7.	Mrs ...
8. Flirtation Waltz ... " Toreador"	8.	
9. Lancers ... " Up West"	9.	
10. Valse ... " Country Girl"	10.	
INTERVAL		
11. Valse ... " Valse Bleu"	11.	Mrs ...
12. Lancers " Toreador"	12.	
13. Barn Dance ... " Down South"	13.	
14. Alberts " Pirates of Penzance"	14.	
15. Flirtation Waltz ... ..." Down the Vale"	15.	
16. Lancers ... " Country Girl"	16.	
17. Valse ... " Three Little Maids"	17.	
18. Alberts ... " Chinese Honeymoon"	18.	
19. Valse ... " Frou-Frou"	19.	
20. Valse & Galop ... " Post Horn"	20.	
EXTRAS		
1. ... 3. ...	1. ... 3. ...	
2. ... 4. ...	2. ... 4. ...	

YOUR WORKING LIFE

The story didn't mention what my grandfather did for a living; so during an interview ensure you ask as many questions as possible.

For example:
What was the occupation of the family?
Did they own a business?
What did they make or manufacture?
Where was the business?
What year did your relative start the business and if no longer in existence, when did they sell it?
How many employees?

Visiting Cards: The two examples below belong to the same person but the address and telephone numbers are different. Note the old telephone number and postcode. When/why did they move from one place to another?

49

Were you employed? In this case take copies of your:

Curriculum Vitae (CV)
Job Description
Contract of employment
Terms and Conditions of Service

First Pay slip - **the example below would have had the person's name included. Notice how much per month this person earned as compared to earnings today (old money - £.s.d).**

First Pay Slip

ADDITIONS CODES		DEDUCTIONS CODES		MARKS & SPENCER LTD.
A - OVERTIME	✳ - REFUND	F - NATIONAL HEALTH BENEFIT		
B - RETROSPECTIVE ADJUSTMENT	D - GRANT	G - WAGES NOT PAID		SALARY ADVICE SLIP
C - WAGES IN LIEU OF HOLIDAYS	E - BONUS	H - RETROSPECTIVE ADJUSTMENT		

BASIC SALARY		ADDITIONS/DEDUCTIONS		GROSS SALARY	EMP. NO.	
£ s. d.	CODE £ s. d.	CODE £ s. d.		£ s. d.		
72 18 4				72 18 4	131	

TAX	NATIONAL INSURANCE	GRAD. INSURANCE	H. S. P.	LOAN REPAYMENTS	TAX CODE	
£ s. d.	£ s. d.	£ s. d.	£ s. d.	£ s. d.		
11 15 0	2 16 4	1 12 2			206	MEN'S SHIRTS

LUCHEON	NAT. SAVINGS		NET PAY	CREDITED TO YOUR ACCOUNT FOR
£ s. d.	£ s. d.		£ s. d.	
			56 14 10	JULY

Long service awards parties or retirement parties.

Make a note of: The names of your colleagues, the date and place where the party was held. If a photograph was taken, name the people. Mention if they were your personal friends, relatives or your colleagues.

WERE YOUR FAMILY IN THE FORCES?

Did any members of your family serve in the forces? According to the story, my uncle Jonathan was killed during the First World War. He joined the First Surrey Rifles and was killed in France (aged 19) on 31 September 1917. Unfortunately the family don't know where he is buried. (See pages 53 and 54).

Ask your relatives whether there are photographs of the family in uniform. Do they have photos of them 'then and now'?

1939-1945 War - First Btn. London Irish Rifles
Served in Palestine, Iraq, North Africa, Sicily, Anzio, Monte Camino,
Catania Plain

SERVICE DETAILS

Keep a note of: Where they served. The name of their regiment and service number. The medals they won. Call up papers. Letters they wrote to their loved ones. Any stories about the war.

AIR-GRAMS

The following are examples of air-grams. These were letters sent both from families to their loved ones serving in the forces or vice versa. As you will see they have been reduced in size (or microfilmed) and have gone through a censor.

(See page 56 for the story behind these.)

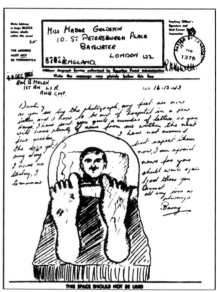

COMMONWEALTH WAR GRAVE COMMISSION

If unfortunately members of your family were killed in action abroad during the First or Second World War and you don't know where they are buried, have a look at the web-site of the Commonwealth War Grave Commission (see page 103). This organisation provides two pages of information on each soldier. The first page shows the **soldier's name, regiment, age and date of death, the name of his parents and the cemetery**.

In Memory of

Lieutenant PETER NATHANIEL MYERS

*4th Regt., Reconnaissance Corps, R.A.C.
who died aged 22 on Tuesday, 7th November 1944.*

Lieutenant MYERS was the son of Harry and Kate Myers, of Bloomsbury, London.

*Remembered with honour
CORIANO RIDGE WAR CEMETERY, Italy.*

*In the perpetual care of
the Commonwealth War Graves Commission*

The second page has additional information showing the **grave reference, instructions on how to get to the cemetery and historical information concerning the battle**.

In Memory of

PETER NATHANIEL MYERS

Lieutenant
262954
4th Regt., Reconnaissance Corps, R.A.C.
who died on
Tuesday, 7th November 1944. Age 22.

Additional Information:	Son of Harry and Kate Myers, of Bloomsbury, London.

Commemorative Information

Cemetery:	CORIANO RIDGE WAR CEMETERY, Italy
Grave Reference/ Panel Number:	XII, D, 3.
Location:	Coriano Ridge War Cemetery is 3.5 kilometres west of Riccione, a seaside resort on the Adriatic coast, and is reached by turning west off the main Rimini/Riccione road, the SS 16, about 1 kilometre north-west of Riccione. At this turning there is a sign leading to the cemetery. Follow it in the direction of Coriano until a T junction is reached, then turn left and after a short distance the cemetery will be found on the right-hand side. The cemetery is permanently open and may be visited anytime.
Historical Information:	Coriano Ridge was the last important ridge in the way of the Allied advance in the Adriatic sector in the autumn of 1944. Its capture was the key to Rimini and eventually to the River Po. German Parachute and Panzer troops, aided by bad weather, resisted all attacks on their positions between 4th and 12th September 1944. On the night of 12th September the Eighth Army re-opened its attack on the Ridge, with the 1st British Armoured Division and the 5th Canadian Armoured Division. This attack was successful in taking the Ridge, but marked the beginning of a week of the heaviest fighting experienced since Cassino, the Eighth Army losing daily some 150 killed, who lie buried in this cemetery. The site for the cemetery was selected by the Army in April 1945 and it was formed by concentrations from the surrounding battlefields. There are now nearly 2,000, 1939-45 war casualties commemorated in this site.

BRITISH JEWRY BOOK OF HONOUR

Look at the British Jewry Book of Honour by Michael Adler as it has lists and photographs of those known to have served during the First World War (JGSGB's library - access for members only). If you visit a military cemetery, take a photograph of the grave and if you have a photograph of the person concerned, mount them next to one another in your family history file.

WAR MEMORIALS

Many synagogues and cemeteries have war memorials - make a point of looking at these when you visit. The Imperial War Museum (address on page 102) is in the process of producing an inventory of all war memorials throughout the UK.

CAMPAIGN STARS, CLASPS AND MEDALS

You may have been handed down the medals which members of your family won during the war. With these came a list - as shown below:

There are books available in the library giving the history of each medal - if you borrow the book, take photocopies of the relevant pages.

Campaign Stars, Clasps and Medals
instituted in recognition of service
in the war of 1939-45

NUMBER OF STARS, MEDALS, CLASPS or EMBLEMS ENCLOSED	5/c'

Order of Wearing	Description of Ribbon	Clasp or Emblem (if awarded)
1 1939-45 Star	Dark blue, red and light blue in three equal vertical stripes. This ribbon is worn with the dark blue stripe furthest from the left shoulder.	Battle of Britain
2 Atlantic Star	Blue, white and sea green shaded and watered. This ribbon is worn with the blue edge furthest from the left shoulder.	Air Crew Europe or France and Germany
3 Air Crew Europe Star	Light blue with black edges and in addition a narrow yellow stripe on either side.	Atlantic or France and Germany
4 Africa Star	Pale buff, with a central vertical red stripe and two narrower stripes, one dark blue, and the other light blue. This ribbon is worn with the dark blue stripe furthest from the left shoulder.	8th Army or 1st Army or North Africa 1942-43
5 Pacific Star	Dark green with red edges, a central yellow stripe, and two narrow stripes, one dark blue and the other light blue. This ribbon is worn with the dark blue stripe furthest from the left shoulder.	Burma
6 Burma Star	Dark blue with a central red stripe and in addition two orange stripes.	Pacific
7 Italy Star	Five vertical stripes of equal width, one in red at either edge and one in green at the centre, the two intervening stripes being in white.	
8 France and Germany Star	Five vertical stripes of equal width, one in blue at either edge and one in red at the centre, the two intervening stripes being in white.	Atlantic
9 Defence Medal	Flame coloured with green edges, upon each of which is a narrow black stripe.	Silver laurel leaves (King's Commendation for brave conduct. Civil)
10 War Medal 1939-45	A narrow central red stripe with a narrow white stripe on either side. A broad red stripe at either edge, and two intervening stripes in blue.	Oak leaf

MEMENTOS

You may find that your family have kept letters or postcards from members of the forces serving abroad.

Below is a cable/telegram, which was sent in 1944 by a soldier to his fiancé. He had trench feet and the telegram is saying that he is now fit and well - **note the censor mark. It also shows the name of the person and address**. There is a story behind every letter. (How did he get trench feet? Where was he serving? Where was he in hospital? Now he is well has he returned to his regiment?) See air-gram on page 52 - this shows him in hospital, so the two documents tie up with one another.

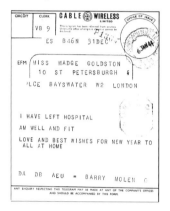

POSTCARDS

This postcard was sent to a boy who was evacuated to a Boarding School in Sussex during the Second World War from his uncle who was serving in the forces in Israel. Note the censor stamps. **Again there will be a story about the soldier and another about the boy.**

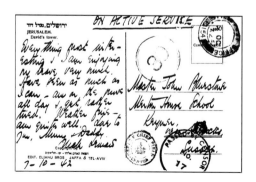

RATION BOOKS
IDENTITY AND ALIEN REGISTRATION

In 1939 petrol rationing started and on the 8 January 1940 food rationing began - for example you were only allowed to buy 4 ozs of butter and 12 ozs sugar with your coupons. Clothing rationing imposed in 1941 ended on the 15 March 1949. The utility scheme in which ready-to-wear clothes were made under a cloth quota system continued. Price control on clothing, however stayed. On the eve of 3 July 1954 men and women ceremonially tore up their ration books in Trafalgar Square as the government announced the end of rationing after 14 years. Clothes and sweet rationing were ended in 1949. Meat was the last to go.

The Food Ration book on the previous page shows: **The year of issue (1953-54), surname and first name and address. In addition, it shows the name of the shop where the coupons could be exchanged for food.**

CLOTHING BOOK

The clothing book example below gives the following details: **holder's name and address and year of issue (1947-48).**

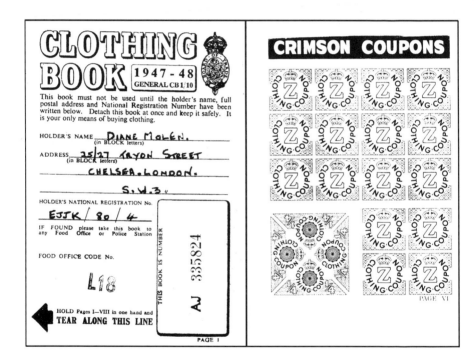

MOTOR FUEL RATION BOOK

The motor fuel ration book below gives the following details: **Registration number of vehicle, date and office of issue, full name and address plus signature.**

LH 854833

Motor Fuel Ration Book

MOTOR CAR
(inc. Tricycle)
not exceeding
1100
C.C.
1 – 9
H.P.

The coupons in this book authorise the furnishing and acquisition of the number of units of motor fuel specified on the coupons. Wt. 33559.

Registered No. of Vehicle	**Registered No. of Vehicle** **LH 854833**
Date and Office of Issue	Date and Office of Issue

This book is the property of Her Majesty's Government

Instructions to Issuing Clerk:

See that the issue of this Ration Book is Recorded on the applicant's registration book.

This portion, after completion, to be detached and forwarded to the Regional Petroleum Officer with Form P 2218

NOT TRANSFERABLE   **LH 854833**

THIS SLIP MUST BE COMPLETED AND ATTACHED TO ANY APPLICATION FOR A SUPPLEMENTARY PETROL ALLOWANCE FOR THE VEHICLE FOR WHICH THIS BOOK WAS ISSUED.

I CERTIFY THAT THE UNDERMENTIONED VEHICLE IS REGISTERED IN THE NAME OF THE PERSON, FIRM OR COMPANY SHOWN BELOW.

Name in full _____
(BLOCK LETTERS)
Address _____

Registered No.   H.P./C.C.
of Vehicle _____   of Vehicle _____

Signature _____

LH 854833   **LH 854833**

1ST MONTH   **1ST MONTH**
NOT TRANSFERABLE   NOT TRANSFERABLE
This coupon is issued under the authority of the Minister of Power   This coupon is issued under the authority of the Minister of Power

Two **N2** Units   Two **N2** Units

Attention is drawn to the provisions and conditions appearing overleaf   Attention is drawn to the provisions and conditions appearing overleaf
REGISTERED No OF VEHICLE   REGISTERED No OF VEHICLE

IDENTITY CARD (National Registration)

The example below shows: **the full name and current postal address. Note it also shows the previous addresses and the card has been date stamped against each address. Plus the fact that the person moved from the first address in 1949 to a new address in 1949 then moved again in 1950 and 1951.**

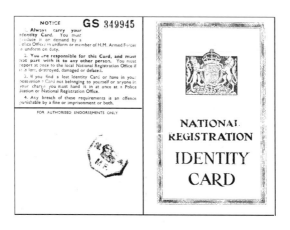

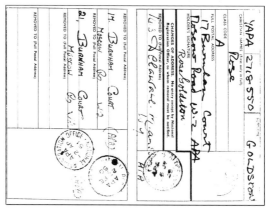

ALIEN REGISTRATION

The Alien Registration identity booklet (on page 61) was issued in 1918. It contains 16 pages, the first page and last pages are shown on page 61.

The second page (shown on page 63) gives the following information: **Surname, First names, Date of Birth, Nationality, Birthplace, Postal Address in this Country, Business Address, Trade, Profession or Employment, Name of Employer, Whether House owner, Tenant, Lodger or Employee at Address.**

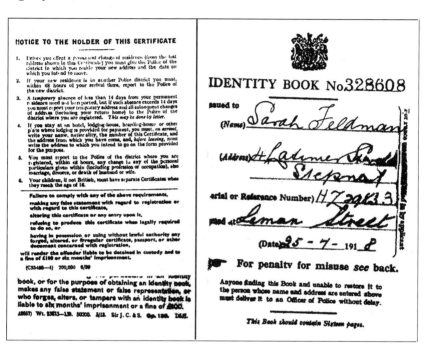

The third page gives: **Particulars of Family - Name of Husband and Children under 18 if in the United Kingdom also Particulars of Service in any Army, Navy or Police Force and any other Government Service.**

The Fourth page gives: **Personal Description eg height, build, hair, distinctive marks, signature of applicant, left thumb print (if unable to sign name in English Characters) and photograph.**

The Fifth page shows: **Nationality at birth, Name of Father, Father's nationality at birth, Maiden name of Mother, Mother's nationality at birth**.

Page Six: **Maiden name of Wife; Nationality of wife/husband at birth, Nationality of Passport, Whether or not absent from the United Kingdom at any time since 4 August 1914, Whether previously possessed an Identity Book**.

Page Seven: **State whether applicant has or has had any male relatives in arms for or against Great Britain and Allies during the present war, State whether convicted of any offences against the Defence of the Realm regulations, the Aliens Restriction Order, or the laws relating to trading with the enemy, Signature of applicant at bottom of page**.

Page Eight: **We, being Natural-born British Subjects and Householders, certify that the declaration on page seven was signed by (insert signature) in our presence and that to the best of our knowledge and belief the foregoing particulars are true (signature and permanent address of two witnesses)**.

Page Nine: **I certify that this identity book was produced to me duly filled up and attested, that the description and photograph (or finger prints) which appear therein are those of (insert name) and that his/her present address is correctly given (signature, rank, police station stamp, police force date and signature or 'mark'**.

Page Ten onwards: **Endorsements and remarks - these include names, sex, year of birth of children**.

1. Surname (*in capitals*) _FELDMAN_

2. Christian names _Sarah_

3. (a) Date of birth _15 June 1867_ (b) Sex _female_

4. (a) Nationality _Russian_

   (b) Birthplace _Bruslov_

Postal Address in this country (*in full*) :—
   (a) Of present residence _4 Fatimer Sb_
   Stepney E1

   (b) Of business _None_

6. (a) Trade, profession or employment* _Household Duties_

   (b) Name of employer* _None_

7. Whether Houseowner, Tenant, Lodger or Employee at Address 5 (a) } _Tenant_

* *If none say 'none.'*

63

NATURALIZATION

The British Nationality and Status of Aliens Act, 1914. Once a person had taken the Oath of Allegiance he/she was entitled to all political and other rights powers and privileges to which a natural-born British subject was entitled. Below is a copy of a certificate of naturalization, the details shown are: **the persons name, address, trade or occupation, place and date of birth, nationality, whether married, name of wife or husband, names and nationality of parents plus names and dates of birth of children. Attached to this form there is an Oath of Allegiance, a police report and various supporting documents.**

Naturalization documentation: the Public Record Office (PRO) holds records dating from the 18th century until 1940. (Address on page 99).

Certificate No. BZ1234

BRITISH NATIONALITY AND STATUS OF ALIENS ACT, 1914
CERTIFICATE OF NATURALIZATION

𝔚𝔥𝔢𝔯𝔢𝔞𝔰   Abraham Goldston

has applied to one of His Majesty's Principal Secretaries of State for a Certificate of Naturalization, alleging with respect to himself the particulars set out below, and has satisfied him that the conditions laid down in the above-mentioned Act for the grant of a Certificate of Naturalization are fulfilled in his case:

And whereas the said **Abraham Goldston** has also applied for the inclusion in accordance with sub-section (I) of section five of the said Act of the names of his children born before the date of this Certificate and being minors, and the Secretary of State is satisfied that the names of his children, as herinafter set out, may properly be included:

Now, therefore in pursuance of the powers conferred on him by the said Act, the Secretary of State grants to the said

Abraham Goldston

this Certificate of Naturalization, and declares that upon taking the Oath of Allegiance within the time and in the manner required by the regulations made in that behalf he shall, subject to the provisions of the said Act, be entitled to all political and other rights powers and privileges, and be subject to all obligations duties and liabilities, to which a natural-born British subject is entitled or subject, and have to all intents and purposes the status of a natural-born British subject.

And the Secretary of State further declares that this Certificate extends to the following minor children of the said **Abraham Goldston**

Joseph Goldston born 31 June 1917
Isaac Goldston born 31 September 1918

In witness whereof I have hereto subscribed my name this 31st day of November 1933.

HOME OFFICE, LONDON   *A. A. Scott*
            Under Secretary of State

PARTICULARS RELATING TO APPLICANT

Full Name:	Abraham Goldston
Address:	1521 Newcastle Road, London, E.1.
Trade or occupation:	Merchant and Buying Commission Agent
Place and date of birth:	Amsterdam, Holland, 30 February 1890
Nationality:	Dutch
Married etc.	Married
Name of wife or husband:	Betje
Names and nationality of parents:	David Goldston and Rose Holland
	Dutch (For Oath see overleaf)
	(Fictitious information given)

64

ON THE STREET WHERE YOU LIVED

If you know where the family lived you may have pictures of the property. As the earlier interview said, my grandmother was born in 1888 and lived at 121 Artillery Passage in the East End of London. Wherever there is a property, make the effort to find out about it.

PROPERTY HISTORY

Visit the site and take a photograph of the property - record the date taken.

Does the property have a history? If so, obtain details.

STREET MAPS

Photocopy a street map, mark the road with a highlighter pen and state the source so that the map can be found in the future. Ensure you include the full address, full date, and the names of all the people living there at the time.

ESTATE AGENTS

If your old house or ancestor's property is up for sale, contact the estate agent and ask for details. You will be surprised how the price has gone up (well hopefully). Some estate agents even show the plan of the inside of the property (*overleaf*).

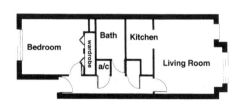

FAMILY ADDRESSES

Make a list in alphabetical order of all the addresses where your family lived. To make a start, details may be taken from your old address books or from birth, marriage and death certificates - as I have said above, do note the dates they lived there. In years to come this will help your relatives when looking up census returns.

CHANGE OF ADDRESS CARDS

Sometimes the card will also show the current address. Note: **the old telephone number and a slightly different post-code to that used today**.

> *On 30 February 1948*
> ### ANDREA AND SIMON
> *will be moving to:*
> *2116 Alexander Road*
> *Maida Vale*
> *London W.9.*
> *Our phone number will still be*
> *(CUN)ningham 6459*

(Fictitious information given)

CENSUS RETURNS - WHAT ARE THEY?

As the story said, my grandmother was born at 121 Artillery Passage in 1888, therefore have a look at the 1891 census for this address. The purpose of Census returns is to compile information about the population and resources of a country. Counts are taken every 10 years. In England & Wales the detailed data is not released for 100 years. The next one due for release is the 1901 census.

The great advantage of looking at census returns is that you can follow developments over a period of time. They also give a picture of the whole family at the time the census was taken. It is very likely you will discover previously unknown relatives. This is why keeping lists of addresses and the dates when your family lived in various properties can be of such value to generations to come. It is a good idea to look through your current or old address books and extract the information into your family history file.

Census returns are held at the Family Record Centre (address on page 99).

Note: The example of the census on the following page shows that between 1861 and 1871 Joshua Barnett's family had three more children. Notice too that in 1861 Joshua Barnett was listed as aged 41 but in the 1871 census he is shown as aged 55! This proves that unfortunately you cannot always rely on the accuracy of these returns.

In addition – the death announcement (on page 87) shows that Nancy Barnett was still living at the same address when she died in 1898 as she was on the 1861 and 1871 census returns (on page 68). Therefore these two documents tie up with one another.

CENSUS

```
                    CENSUS FOR 1851 OR OTHER CENSUS YEARS:-
YEAR:     1851                 PRO REFERENCE:            HD107/1524
COUNTY:   MIDDLESEX            REGISTRAR'S DISTRICT:      EAST LONDON
                              SUB - DISTRICT:            ST.BOTOLPH
ENUMERATION DISTRICT:  1G     TOWN,VILLAGE OR HAMLET OF: ST.BOTOLPH,
```

ROAD,STREET ETC & No. OR NAME OF HOUSE:	NAME AND SURNAME OF EARCH PERSON:	RELATION TO HEAD OF FAMILY	CONDITION	AG
1 HARROW ALLEY	AARON SYMONS	HEAD	MARRIED	81
	ELIZABETH SYMONS	WIFE	MARRIED	65
	ESTHER SYMONS	DAUGHTER	UNMARRIED	20
	FRANCES SYMONS	DAUGHTER	MARRIED	30
	ISAAC SYMONS	SON	MARRIED	41
	LEWIS SYMONS	SON	UNMARRIED	32

```
                    CENSUS FOR 1871 OR OTHER CENSUS YEARS:-
YEAR:     1871                 PRO REFERENCE:            RG10/412
COUNTY:   MIDDLESEX            REGISTRAR'S DISTRICT:      LONDON CITY
                              SUB - DISTRICT:            ST.BOTOLPH
ENUMERATION DISTRICT:  3      TOWN,VILLAGE OR HAMLET OF: ALDGATE
```

ROAD,STREET ETC & No. OR NAME OF HOUSE:	NAME AND SURNAME OF EARCH PERSON:	RELATION TO HEAD OF FAMILY	CONDITION	AG
9 HARROW ALLEY	JOSHUA BARNETT	HEAD	MARRIED	55
	NANCY BARNETT	WIFE	MARRIED	47
	BARON BARNETT	SON	UNMARRIED	22
	ABRAHAM BARNETT	SON	UNMARRIED	21
	MARY BARNETT	DAUGHTER	UNMARRIED	20
	ELAIS BARNETT	SON	UNMARRIED	19
	FANNY BARNETT	DAUGHTER		16
	ASHER BARNETT	SON		14
	ELIZABETH BARNETT	DAUGHTER		12
	MARK BARNETT	SON		11
	SAMUEL BARNETT	SON		9
	REBECCA BARNETT	DAUGHTER		7
	ISABELLA BARNETT	DAUGHTER		4

```
                    CENSUS FOR 1861 OR OTHER CENSUS YEARS:-
YEAR:     1861                 PRO REFERENCE:            RG9/210
COUNTY:   MIDDLESEX            REGISTRAR'S DISTRICT:      EAST LONDON
                              SUB - DISTRICT:            ST.BOTOLPH
ENUMERATION DISTRICT:  2      TOWN,VILLAGE OR HAMLET OF: ST.BOTOLPH
```

ROAD,STREET ETC & No. OR NAME OF HOUSE:	NAME AND SURNAME OF EARCH PERSON:	RELATION TO HEAD OF FAMILY	CONDITION	AG
9 HARROW ALLEY	JOSHUA BARNETT	HEAD	MARRIED	41
	NANCY BARNETT	WIFE	MARRIED	37
	LEWIS BARNETT	SON	UNMARRIED	16
	BARON BARNETT	SON		12
	ABRAHAM BARNETT	SON		11
	MARY BARNETT	DAUGHTER		10
	ELAIS BARNETT	SON		8

RENT BOOKS

Did your family rent accommodation? Below is an example of a 1911 rent book. The writing is very small but the tenant, Mr. Holland, paid 11/6d (Eleven old shillings and six old pence per week). **The document shows Mr. Holland's address, the year he rented the accommodation and the name and address of the landlord or agent. Plus all the rules and regulations**.

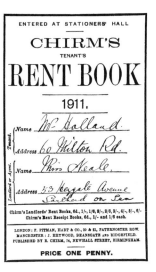

FREEMASONS

Were any of your family freemasons? If so include photographs and details of their Masonic lodge.

The United Grand Lodge of England (address on page 99) has a very large library and although they take a very long time to reply to any request, they are extremely helpful if you decide to contact them.

The information I have received about a particular relative is as follows:

Lodge name	Date raised
Lodge number	Age
Lodge area	Address
Date initiated	Occupation
Date passed	Date of Death
	Offices Held

The photograph below shows an inscription on this Masonic insignia:

YOUR PETS!

Don't forget to include details of your pets, after all, they are part of your family. Did your pet have kittens or puppies? What were your thoughts for seeing the birth? Perhaps they were 'rescued' from one of the rescue organisation. Did they win an award - Crufts? Were their photos in the newspapers?

Pet vaccination cards, these too will have **your pet's name and the dates vaccinated plus your home address (which will indicate the date you lived at this particular address)**.

Did you keep the copy of your dog licence? Notice this shows: **Name and address of owner and the date they lived at this address.** The licence was for one dog.

(Fictitious information given)

71

SPECIAL OCCASIONS

In the story, did my grandmother Miriam get a valentine from David? This we do not know. However, if you do receive a valentine or greetings card from an unknown or known admirer, and it was a very special one, do keep it.

This very romantic valentine card was written in February 1900, to the man shown in the photograph on page 18 – therefore the two documents tie up with one another (original on next page).

TO MY VALENTINE

IF YOU LOVE ME LOVE ME TRUE, PLEASE RETURN THE BOW OF BLUE
IF OF ME YOU ONLY THINK, PLEASE RETURN THE BOW OF PINK
IF YOU HATE ME LET IT BE SEEN, BY SENDING BACK THE BOW OF GREEN
IF FOR ME THERE IS SOME HOPE, PLEASE RETURN THE HELIOTROPE
IF YOU WOULD OUR LOVE UNITE, PLEASE RETURN THE BOW OF WHITE
IF FOR ME YOUR LOVE IS DEAD, PLEASE RETURN THE BOW OF RED
IF YOU LOVE ME AS OF OLD, PLEASE RETURN THE BOW OF GOLD
IF YOU LOVE ANOTHER PARTY, PLEASE RETURN THE BOW OF KHAKI
IF YOU DO NOT CARE A JOT, PLEASE RETURN THE BLOOMING LOT

You will note (on the next page) that the blue bow is missing.

To My Valentine

If you love me love me true
Please return the bow of Blue.

If of me you only think
Please return the bow of Pink

If you hate me let it be seen.
By sending back the bow of Green.

If for me there is some hope
Please return the Heliotrope

If you would our love unite
Please return the bow of White.

If for me your love is dead.
Please return the bow of red.

If you love me as of old.
Please return the bow of Gold

If you love another party
Please return the bow of Khaki

If you do not care a jot.
Please return the Blooming Lot

73

BIRTHDAYS

Whether it is your first birthday or your 100th make sure that your special cards are kept and photographs taken. Below is a photograph of a relative taken at her 90th birthday party plus a photograph of her cake. As I have said earlier, it is important to recognise the different stages of your life and record them.

RELIGIOUS OCCASIONS - SIMCHAT TORAH

Simchat Torah (Rejoicing of the Law) marks the completion of the 1 year cycle of the reading of the Torah (Law). But since the Torah reading should be continuous, as soon as the final portion of the Law is read, a second Scroll is opened and a new cycle is begun by reading the first part of Genesis. The male members of the congregation who are honoured by being called up to the Reading of the Law are designated 'Chatan Torah' (Bridegroom of the Law) and 'Chatan Bereshit' (Bridegroom of the Beginning). On the next page are examples of the certificates they receive which show **the** person's English name (sometimes the Hebrew name too), whether he was Chatan Torah or Bereshit, the English and Hebrew dates, name of synagogue and the signatures of the Ministers or Wardens.

WEDDINGS

WEDDING INVITATION

Keep a copy of the invitation and note the details.

On the following invitation is shown: **the names of both parents, the bride and bridegroom, date and time of the wedding, name and address of the synagogue, address and details of where the reception is to be held and the addresses of both the bride and bridegroom**.

Susan & Alan Cohen
with
Helen & David Levy

have pleasure in inviting you
to the marriage of their children

Sandra
and
Brian

on Sunday 30 February 1970
Ceremony 3.30 pm
at Stanmore Synagogue, London Road,
Stanmore, Middlesex
Buffet and Ball 8 to 11 pm
at the Royal Majestic Suite, Willesden Lane, N.W.6

R.S.V.P.
Bride   *Bridegroom*
1489 Gordon Avenue   *2606 London Road*
Stanmore, Middx.   *Edgware, Middx.*

(Fictitious information given)

MARRIAGE AUTHORISATION

This is an example of a marriage authorisation. This document gives permission for the couple to marry under the auspices of a Synagogue - the example below was issued by the United Synagogue. The document gives a lot of information. It shows the **date of application, date of marriage, English and Hebrew names of the bridegroom, his address, place of birth, whether married before and the names of any brothers.** In addition, it gives the **English and Hebrew name of the bride, her address, place of birth, whether married before, the name of the synagogue, the time of the ceremony and the name of the officiant.**

All of this information should be added to your file and to your address list. Addresses and the dates when they lived there, as I have said earlier, are so important to keep for future generations should they wish to follow them up.

No. 439

Date of Application ... November 23rd 1891.

Date of Marriage ... December 24th 1891.

חתן ... Joseph Goldston

Address ... 69 Well Street Plymouth

Native of ... England   Certificate? ...

Married before? ... No   Related to Bride? ...

Brothers (if any) ...

Reside in ...

כלה ... Ada Lewisohn

Address ... 36 Pembridge Villas Bayswater W

Native of ... Germany   Certificate? ...

Married before ... No

Synagogue ... Bayswater

Place of Celebration ...

Hour ... 3

Name of Celebrant ... The Chief Rabbi

❖ Special Remark ...

Signature ...

PHOTOGRAPHS

In addition to photographs of the bride and groom there will be other photographs taken. It is a good idea to mount the photograph of the bride and groom together with a copy of their wedding invitation in your family history file.

OLD WEDDING GROUP PHOTOGRAPHS

From such photos it is important to observe the fashion of the day. Try to identify the people in the photograph and write the details and date taken on the back or as the example below shows. If you are artistic, you can trace the outlines of the people on the photo, then number them and write below the names against the numbers.

The bride in the photograph below wrote the Valentine card shown on page 73 to her then boyfriend, now bridegroom. Therefore these two documents tie up with one another.

MARRIAGE BETWEEN NANCY BARNETT
AND MAURICE BENJAMIN
17 JUNE 1903

Top Row (left to right)
(5) Rose Barnett
(6) Miriam Barnett
(7) Aunt Esther
(8) Aunt Kate

Second Row (left to right)
(5) Isaac Goldston
(7) Aaron (Harry) Barnett

Third Row (left to right)
(1) Baron Barnett (Bride' father)
(2) Agnes Barnett (Bride' mother)
    (nee Nunes-Martines)
(3) Maurice Benjamin (Bridegroom)
(4) Nancy Barnett (Bride)

Fourth Row (left to right)
(3) Agnes Israel (Bridesmaid with
    her hair in ringlets)

ENGAGEMENT ANNOUNCEMENT

Record the details of the announcement in the newspapers: The example below shows the **full names of both parties, both sets of parents and grandparents. Note that Simon is the eldest son, therefore he has younger brothers**.

**KAREN SUSAN COHEN and
SIMON EDWARD LEVY**

Both families are delighted to announce the engagement of Karen, daughter of Joan and Charles Cohen, granddaughter of Elizabeth Cohen and the late George Cohen to Simon, eldest son of Judith and Sidney Levy.

(Fictitious information given)

MARRIAGE CERTIFICATE

If you are lucky as I have been (in the interview) you will not only have been given the date and where your grandparents married, which was 30 February 1911 at Bevis Marks Synagogue, but also a copy of the marriage certificate. **For information**, Bevis Marks have published many of their historical records (Births, Circumcisions, Marriages and Deaths) in book form - these maybe purchased by writing to: The Spanish & Portuguese Jews' Congregation (address on page 101).

You are now married to the man of your dreams - you have a copy of your marriage certificate. This is a legal document and should be kept safely. As with your birth certificate, there is a lot of information given: The certificate on the next page shows the **date and place of the marriage, names and ages of the couple, occupation, addresses, names and occupations of fathers and witnesses. In addition, you will notice that the bride could not either read or write or perhaps she couldn't understand English as she has put a cross where her signature should be and against this is written 'the mark of**

Nancy Ellis'. As with the birth certificate, take an A4 photocopy and file it under the 'marriage section' of your file. Extract as much information and add to your family history file.

Copies of marriage certificates: the public search rooms at the Family Record Centre (address on page 99) have the indexes from 1837 - present. Certificates have to be ordered and there is a charge.

Marriage Certificate

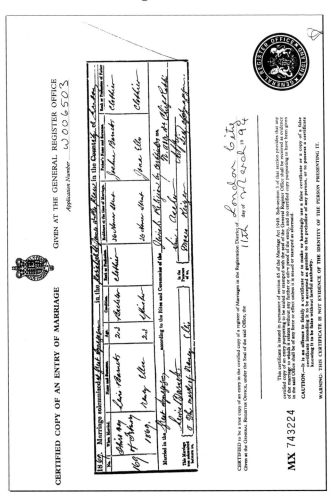

Jewish weddings result in two pieces of paper - a marriage certificate and the Ketubah (see below or glossary on page 105).

KETUBAH

The Ketubah is the Jewish marriage contract. A document in Aramaic read at the marriage service, an abstract of which is generally printed on the other side in English, and which contains a statement of the obligations of a husband and wife towards one another.

If you have copies of both certificates it is a good idea to keep them safely together. However, do photocopy the Ketubah and include it with the copy of your marriage certificate in your file. Remember to reduce the copies in size to A4 in order to fit into your folder.

This example indicates that the bride was a widow.

PLACE OF WORSHIP

If the place of worship is a very old and beautiful one take photos of the interior.

TABLE PLAN

After many hours of deciding who will sit next to who, which member of the family is not speaking to another and who you would like your single best friend to be sitting next to in order for the next marriage to take place, keeping a copy of the table plan is a good way of remembering who came to your wedding. The plans are usually in strict alphabetical order.

(Fictitious information given)

TABLE PLAN

Table Number	Name
4	Aarons, Susan
8	Black, Rosalind
5	Gold, David
9	Harris, Annie

MENU

Keep a copy of the menu, which often shows the names of the people who made speeches and of course a reminder of the cuisine.

(Fictitious information given)

TOASTS

Her Majesty the Queen
Proposed by   Mr. Jack Levy

The President and the State of Israel
Proposed by   Mr. Charles Jay

The Bride and Bridegroom
Proposed by   Mr. John Conroy
Response by   The Bridegroom

Your Host
Mr. Barry Gold

Indicate how these people are related to you.

Save the goodies, which are left on the tables for example matchboxes, Grace after Meals booklets, yarmulka, menu etc. They nearly always have information on them.

WEDDING LISTS

It will be great fun for future generations to see the wedding gifts you received and who gave them - so keep a copy of your wedding list.

SILVER WEDDING

25 years have gone by, your children have grown up and you are now celebrating your silver wedding. Unfortunately, a lot of the family who were at your wedding will no longer be with you. Remember to keep copies of your invitation, the table plan and photos of your friends and family who came plus of course, a photograph of your cake.

BEREAVEMENT

You have lived a very active and enjoyable life, but everything unfortunately must come to an end. You will have recorded your life for generations to come and this will be greatly appreciated by future family historians.

Sadly you have died and the last piece of paper recording your life will be the death certificate.

DEATH CERTIFICATES

U.K death certificates show the **date and place of death, name, sex, age, occupation, cause of death, name and address and relationship of informant**. Please note that UK death certificates do not give a place of burial or parents' names as do many American ones. Your family should keep a copy of this certificate in alphabetical order in your file under the 'deaths section' and record the information in your family tree. (See example on the next page)

STONE SETTING (Consecration of a Tombstone)

It is usual in the Jewish religion to consecrate the tombstone of a relative a year after burial (or slightly earlier if required). If the family have put a notification of the stone setting in the Jewish Chronicle or other Regional newspapers, a copy should be placed in your file. **The details will give the deceased's name, the date, place and time of the stone setting.**

> **LEVY. The memorial stone in loving memory of Charles Levy will be consecrated at Willesden Cemetery on Sunday 30 February 1908 at 11 am**

(Fictitious information given)

Death Certificate

CERTIFIED COPY OF AN ENTRY OF DEATH

Given at the GENERAL REGISTER OFFICE, LONDON.

Application Number 789411

REGISTRATION DISTRICT Hackney

1968 . **DEATH** in the Sub-district of Shoreditch in the London Borough of Hackney

No.	When and where died	Name and surname	Sex	Age	Occupation	Cause of death	Signature, description, and residence of informant	When registered	Signature of registrar
224	Sixteenth August 1968 Metropolitan Hospital Hackney	Herman Ernest Spear	Male	74 years	of 17 Evelyn Court Amhurst Road E.8. Theatre Advertising Agent (retired)	1 (a) Myocardial infarction (b) Respiratory failure (c) Chronic bronchitis Certified by P J Bindley Wadson m8	L Spear Widow of deceased 17 Evelyn Court Amhurst Road E.8	Sixteenth August 1968	F.W. Cotton Registrar

CERTIFIED to be a true copy of an entry in the certified copy of a Register of Deaths in the District above mentioned.
Given at the GENERAL REGISTER OFFICE, LONDON, under the Seal of the said Office, the 12th day of November 1986.

This certificate is issued in pursuance of the Births and Deaths Registration Act 1953. Section 34 provides that any certified copy of an entry purporting to be sealed or stamped with the seal of the General Register Office shall be received as evidence of the birth or death to which it relates without any further or other proof of the entry, and no certified copy purporting to have been given in the said Office shall be of any force or effect unless it is sealed or stamped as aforesaid.

CAUTION—It is an offence to falsify a certificate or to make or knowingly use a false certificate or a copy of a false certificate intending it to be accepted as genuine to the prejudice of any person or to possess a certificate knowing it to be false without lawful authority.

DA 801160

Form A504 Dd. 8924033 12M Mar./'88 (1327748)

85

CONDOLENCES

There are sometimes entries thanking family and friends for letters of condolence, these too will give some information.

IN MEMORIAM

Notices of remembrance are also put into the Jewish Chronicle or other Regional Newspapers.

COHEN Charles. In loving memory of our dear father who passed away on the 30 February 1926 and our brother Simon who passed away 31 April 1935. Forever in our thoughts.
Angela, Joe and family

(Fictitious information given)

NEWSPAPER ANNOUNCEMENTS (DEATH)

The family should keep copies of all newspaper announcements. The example (on page 87) was taken from the Jewish Chronicle in 1898 the details include, the **name of the deceased, the date they died, the address where they died, the name of their husband, their age and the names and addresses of all the children**. All these details should be added to your tree. In 1898, it wouldn't have crossed our ancestor's minds as to how important and helpful this detailed information would be in the future. **Have a look at the 1901 census returns for this period (which are now available) and note who else lived at these addresses. In addition, you may find out who Mrs. White, Mrs. Taylor, Mrs. Wolfers and Mrs. Benabo are and how they are related to you as the surnames are those of their husbands. In those days, for example, Mrs. J. Simmonds - the 'J' would have been the initial of her husband.**

JEWISH CHRONICLE
FRIDAY 27 MAY 1898
DEATH ANNOUNCEMENT

BARNETT: On Friday, the 20th May, 104A Bridge Street, Burdett Road, NANCY, relict of the late JOSHUA BARNETT, of 9 Harrow Alley, in her 75th year; mother of Baron Barnett, $12\frac{1}{2}$ Artillery Passage, E.C., Elias Barnett, 26 Cutler Street, City; Mrs.White, 5 Tenter Street North, Mrs. Taylor, 120 Antil Road, Bow; Mrs. Wolfers, 104D, Bridge Street; Mark Barnett, 60 Landseer Road, N., Mrs. Benabo, 17 White Horse Street, Bow; Abraham Barnett and Mrs. J. Simmonds, 12 Ormside Street, S.E.

Deeply mourned by her loving children, sisters, grandchildren, relatives and a large circle of friends.

May her dear soul rest in peace. Amen.

Foreign papers please copy

CEMETERIES

When tracing your ancestors it is most rewarding when you visit their grave to read the headstone inscription - some graves give you **the full names of the family**. Other graves may show an **additional name listed** and another that **a member of the family has died**. This information may help you ascertain a relative's age. In some cases, the headstone may show the **address of the deceased** (as example on next page.)

Photograph the grave (check with cemetery office first) and keep a note of the name of the cemetery, the section, row and grave number and when the photo was taken. The grave will also have the person's **Hebrew name and that of his/her father**. It may also indicate whether the deceased was a Cohen or a Levi by the symbol on the grave, as shown below.

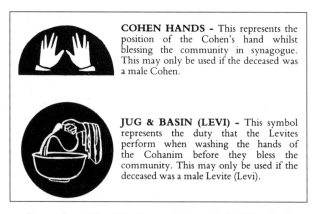

COHEN HANDS - This represents the position of the Cohen's hand whilst blessing the community in synagogue. This may only be used if the deceased was a male Cohen.

JUG & BASIN (LEVI) - This symbol represents the duty that the Levites perform when washing the hands of the Cohanim before they bless the community. This may only be used if the deceased was a male Levite (Levi).

Reproduced by kind permission of A. Elfes Ltd.

GRAVE LOCATION CARDS

If you visit a cemetery and do not know where your family is buried, the cemetery office will give you a card showing the following details: **the section, the row, the grave number and the date of interment** (example below). **Notice on this card that trolley buses were running.**

ק"ק כנסת ישראל

United Synagogue

Telephone : WILlesden 0394.

Resident Superintendent—E. PHILLIPS.

WILLESDEN CEMETERY,
Glebe Road, Pound Lane, N.W.10.

The Cemetery is open daily (Sabbaths & Holydays excepted) **9 a.m. — 6 p.m.** or until dusk if earlier. Entrance in Glebe Road, a turning off Pound Lane, within a few yards of the junction of Pound Lane and Willesden High Road.

LONDON TRANSPORT FACILITIES.

Nearest Stations : <u>Willesden Green</u> (Metro.)—then by Trolley-bus 660, 664 or 666 to corner of Pound Lane. <u>Dollis Hill</u> (Metro.—five minutes' walk).

Buses : Nos. 1 and 8 stop at corner of Pound Lane. Nos. 8, 46 and 52 stop at corner of Dudden Hill Lane (two minutes' walk).

Trolley Buses : 660, 664 or 666 to Pound Lane.

THE INDICATIONS OF THE GRAVE OF THE LATE

Kate Myers are

Section *AX* Row *18* No. *831* Date of Interment *10/5/46*

Any officer or employee receiving a gratuity is liable to dismissal.
For reservation of grave, apply to Superintendent or Sexton.

Please see other side

Allow time for reflection at each grave to remember the life of your relative, after all it may be many years before another relative visits this grave. If there is a **cemetery plan** available, keep this too, so in years to come the graves can be found. The United Synagogue's web-site (see page 103) has plans of all its cemeteries.

All this information should be added to your family history file.

Additional copies of death certificates may be obtained from the Family Record Centre (address on page 99).

WILLS

According to the original interview, my mother said that my aunt Agnes left a lot of money in her will.

The will of an ancestor may contain a great amount of unexpected information, which will be most welcome in providing a fuller picture of his or her life than any other formal document is likely to do. A will can bring you closer to your ancestor. When reading it you may come across some odd bequests - difficult to understand why certain items were given. **In addition, the will could give a complete list of other relatives, for example, their children, grandchildren, aunts, uncles and cousins with all their addresses.** This information is invaluable and should be recorded in your family history file. Remember to take a photocopy of the will.

Look at probate records.

Wills are held at the Principal Registry of the Family Division (records were previously held at Somerset House). From 1858, England and Wales may be seen at the Family Record Centre (both addresses are on page 99).

The example is not an actual will as there are no witness signatures.

I LEWIS BARNETT of Fifty four Lincoln Street Bow in the County of Middlesex hereby revoke all wills and testamentary instruments heretofore by me made and declare this to be my last will whereof I appoint Baron Barnett of 12½ Artillery Passage Bishopsgate <u>and</u>   <u>of</u>   to be the EXECUTOR I direct my executor to pay my just debts and funeral and testamentary expenses I give and bequeath to my wife Nancy Barnett al my household furniture bedding &c I give and bequeath to my brother Asher Barnett his wife or child the sum of twenty five pounds I give and bequeath to my nephews Louis Barnett son of Baron Louis Barnett son of Mark & Louis Ellis son of Solomon Ellis the sum of twenty five pounds to each I give and bequeath to each of my nephews Benjamin and Joseph Benjamin the sum of twenty five pounds and the residue to my wife Nancy Barnett - LEWIS BARNETT - Signed by said Lewis Barnett the testator in our joint presence and signed by us at his request in his presence and in the presence of each other October 12th 1896 - Baron Barnett General Dealer 12½ Artillery Passage Bishopsgate - Agnes Barnett Married 12½ Artillery Passage Bishopsgate

ON the 13th day of August 1896 Probate of this will was granted to Baron Barnett the sole executor

OTHER ITEMS IN
YOUR HOME

DRIVING LICENCES

You may have found some old full and provisional driving licences - as the example below shows they will give the following details: **Full name and address and the date of the licence.** Today's licences also show the persons date of birth.

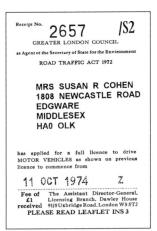

(Fictitious information given)

DONOR CARDS/IN CASE OF EMERGENCY CARDS

Did any of your family carry organ donor cards, or in case of emergency cards? Perhaps they were blood donors? If so they would have been issued with a card or record book. The example of a blood group card (on page 92) shows **the person's blood group, full name and address and date of birth**.

```
NATIONAL BLOOD TRANSFUSION SERVICE                    N.B.T.S.40
                                                      (Rev. 1960)
     North London Blood Transfusion Centre,
              Deansbrook Road,
            Edgware, Middlesex.        Tel.  Edgware 5511

                    This card to be given to:

GROUP                                              Date of Birth
              MRS SUSAN R COHEN
  AB          1808 NEWCASTLE ROAD
              EDGWARE                              Lab. Ref. No.
              MIDDLESEX
Rh Positive   HA0 OLK


                                                   Director.
                                                   P.T.O.
```

(Fictitious information given)

MEDICAL/VACCINATION CARD

Each person has his/her medical card, which means you are registered with a doctor. As you will see from the example below it gives **the person's National Health Service (NHS) number, date of birth, full name and address and the name of his/her doctor**.

```
            NATIONAL HEALTH SERVICE
                MEDICAL CARD
                ISSUED BY THE

         Hertfordshire Family Practitioner Committee
              14 Parliament Square
              HERTFORD, SG14 1ED

Please quote this number if you write to the Family Practitioner Committee   DATE OF BIRTH
N.H.S. Number

                                                      Please notify the
Mr., Mrs., Miss., Ms., .............................  Family Practitioner
                                                       Committee of
Address .............................................  changes of name
                                                       or address and
  ...................................................    return this
                                                       card to them.
  ................................ Postcode .........  Make sure you tell
                                                      your doctor, too.

Dr: .................................................   HT
  ..................................................
  ........................Postcode ..................
```

APPOINTMENT CARDS

Medical appointment cards - **these will all have the date of your appointment, your full name, address and sometimes date of birth. (The date of appointment will indicate the date you lived at the address shown).**

HEREDITARY DISEASES

It is quite interesting to note whether there were hereditary diseases in your family for example Muscular Dystrophy - this disease is inherited through a recessive, sex-linked gene so that only males are affected and only females can pass on the disease.

OLD ENVELOPES

These are very interesting both from the point of view of the stamps plus they **will indicate from the postmark the date the person lived at the address shown. The example below shows the date as 1940.**

BILLS, INVOICES AND DELIVERY NOTES

Electricity, Gas, Water, Telephone bills, the local shops etc, will all have an **address and date on them, notice the old telephone number. In addition, if the owner of the shop on the next page is a relative, note he has a son - perhaps they lived on the premises - if there is a date, check census returns**

(depending on date - if published) to find out his name and that of any other members of the family.

Telephone: RENown 2017

H. GREENMAN & SON
Fulham Bakeries Ltd.
English & Continental Bakers
67 LANGFORD ROAD, FULHAM, S.W.6

M _____

_____

_____ *196* __

BANK, POST OFFICE, BUILDING SOCIETY

All savings account books will show the **person's full name, address and a date**.

DISABLED DRIVERS

If you belong to the Orange Badge Scheme for disabled drivers, inside the orange booklet will show **your name, a photograph of yourself and a date**.

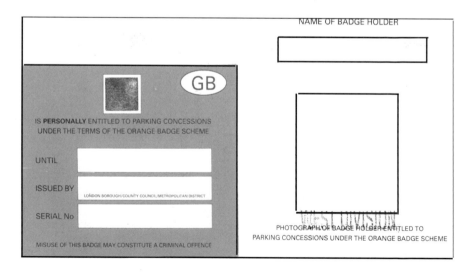

NAME OF BADGE HOLDER

GB

IS **PERSONALLY** ENTITLED TO PARKING CONCESSIONS UNDER THE TERMS OF THE ORANGE BADGE SCHEME

UNTIL

ISSUED BY
LONDON BOROUGH/COUNTY COUNCIL/METROPOLITAN DISTRICT

SERIAL No

MISUSE OF THIS BADGE MAY CONSTITUTE A CRIMINAL OFFENCE

PHOTOGRAPH OF BADGE HOLDER ENTITLED TO PARKING CONCESSIONS UNDER THE ORANGE BADGE SCHEME

P.60 - END OF YEAR SALARY FORM

These will have your **name, address and the year shown**.

PENSION

When you reach retirement age and are eligible to receive a pension, there will be the following details on your pension book: **your full name and address, the date, the day your pension is paid, the post office concerned and your National Insurance Number. In addition there will be details on your pension payment advice.**

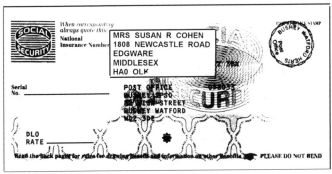

(Fictitious information given)

INLAND REVENUE - TAX FORMS

The tax form will show your **name, address and year**.

PREMIUM BONDS

This premium bond holder's card will show **the holder's number and name and address.**

(Fictitious information given)

Premium Bond Holder's Card - PART B

Holder's Number

Please Note

Keep this card (Part B) in a safe place with your bonds for further use. Do not complete it until you need to send it to the Bonds and Stock Office (address below).

Change of Normal Address
If you change your name and address it is *important* that you complete the reverse of this card (Part B) and send it to the Bonds and Stock Office at the address shown below. You will receive a new Holder's Card bearing your new name/address.

MRS SUSAN R COHEN
1808 NEWCASTLE ROAD
EDGWARE
MIDDLESEX
HA0 OLK

The Holder's Number and Name and Address above are recorded in the Bonds and Stock Office for your Premium Savings Bonds.

Department for National Savings
Bonds and Stock Office
Lytham St. Annes
Lancs FYO 1YN

DIARIES

The following personal information will be found in the front of most diaries:

Name: _____

Address: _____

Telephone No: _____

Business Address: _____

Business Telephone No: _____

National Insurance No: _____

Car Registration No: _____

AA/RAC Membership No: _____

Passport No: _____

IN THE CASE OF AN ACCIDENT PLEASE INFORM

Name: _____

Address: _____

Telephone No: _____

Relationship: _____

Personal Doctor: _____

Address: _____

Telephone No: _____

Blood Group: _____

Allergies: _____

TELEPHONE DIRECTORIES

Perhaps you have an unusual surname, if so, look in the telephone directories to see whether there is someone with the same name. Write and ask if they could help you with your family tree - to ensure a reply, remember to send a stamped addressed envelope.

If you have no luck, you can always visit the British Telecom Archives (address on page 99).

VEHICLE REGISTRATION (V5)

The vehicle registration form (on page 98) shows **your name and address and date of registration of your car** (this detail will confirm the date you were living at this address) plus other details relating to your car. However, when you sell your car, the bottom part of the form has to be sent to the DVLC and the top half given to the new owner. Before parting with the document, take a photocopy and keep it in your file as the details maybe of interest to people in years to come.

INSURANCE POLICIES

Old insurance policies are interesting to look at as they give **the name of the insurer, his or her address, by trades and by the policy number and how much insurance cover they had**. Old insurance records may be seen in the manuscript section of the Guildhall Library (address on page 100). By their use it is possible to distinguish individuals bearing the same name one from the other, follow their movements from place to place and link generations when the owner dies and a policy is taken over. (*Shemot, October 1997, Vol. 5, No. 3 p9 – Jewish Names in Insurance Records by George Rigal*)

(Fictitious information given)

Department of Transport   XYZ 123456789

Vehicle Registration Document

V5
Rev. Nov/88

Registration Mark	**CAT 1234 AA** 00	Validation Character 0

MRS SUSAN R COHEN
1808 NEWCASTLE ROAD
EDGWARE
MIDDLESEX
HA0 0LK   12345

PLEASE QUOTE THE REGISTRATION MARK
IN ALL CORRESPONDENCE

This is the Registration Document for the vehicle described opposite. The person named above is the Registered Keeper of the vehicle (the person recorded as keeping it). **The Registered Keeper is not necessarily the legal owner.** This Document is issued by the Driver and Vehicle Licensing Centre on behalf of the Secretary of State for Transport. Police officers and certain officers of the Department of Transport may require you to produce it for inspection at any reasonable time. **YOU ARE REQUIRED BY LAW TO NOTIFY CHANGES TO THE NAME AND ADDRESS OR VEHICLE PARTICULARS PRINTED ON THIS DOCUMENT AS SOON AS THEY OCCUR - SEE OVERLEAF.** For further information about registering, licensing, insuring and testing your vehicle, please ask at a post office or Vehicle Registration Office for leaflet V100.

Taxation Class	PRIVATE/LIGHT GOODS (PLG)
Make	LAND ROVER
Model/Type	110 DEFENDER TURBO DIES ESTATE
Colour(s)	RED
Type of Fuel	HEAVY OIL
VIN/Chassis/Frame No	CATRW0123456789
Engine No.	0123456789
Cylinder Capacity	2495 CC
Seating Capacity	
Taxable Weight	
Date of Registration	08 03 91
Last Change of Keeper	
No. of Former Keepers	NONE

1. DECLARED NEW AT FIRST REGISTRATION IN GREAT BRITAIN BY MANUFACTURER/SOLE IMPORT CONCESSIONAIRE.
2. IF YOU SELL THE VEHICLE FILL-IN AND RETURN THE TEAR-OFF SLIP BELOW.
3. IF YOU ARE THE NEW KEEPER AND YOUR NAME IS NOT SHOWN ABOVE TELL US NOW BY FILLING IN THE BACK OF THIS FORM. WE WILL THEN SEND YOU A NEW DOCUMENT IN YOUR NAME.

Doc Ref No. 0123 456 7890
12 03 91

32

CAT 1234 AA	000

Notification of Sale or Transfer

If you sell or transfer the vehicle to someone else. **COMPLETE AND DETACH** this section and send it to DVLC SWANSEA SA99 1AR. Please do this at once - it is in your own interest to do so. Give the top part of this document to the new keeper so that he can use it to notify that he has acquired the vehicle.

V5/1
Rev. Nov/88

Registration Mark	CAT 1234 AA	000	000

Date of Sale or Transfer		Official Use Only	

If you have sold or transferred the vehicle to a motor dealer or insurance company, tick here

I sold/transferred this vehicle to the person whose name and address I have written opposite, on the date I have given above. I have also given him/her the top portion of this document.

Signature _____

NOTE: The new keeper must also notify the change in Section 1 overleaf; otherwise a new Registration Document will not be issued.

Name and Address of new Keeper or dealer acquiring vehicle

Mr	1	Mrs	2	Miss	3	Please tick box or give other title below

Other title e.g. Dr., Rev., or company name

Christian or forenames

Surname

Address

Post Town

Postcode

USEFUL ADDRESSES

Once you have gathered all your family documentation, it is now the time to decide what additional documents you require. If you are unable to visit resource centres, you can always write, fax or e-mail them.

Resource	Address	Telephone/Fax/E-mail
Old Telephone Directories	British Telecom Archives, 3rd Floor, Holborn Telephone Exchange, 268-270 High Holborn, London, WC1V 7EE	Tel: 020 7492 8792 (Help Desk) Fax: 020 7242 1967 E-Mail: hayda@boat.bt.com
Vital Records (England & Wales) Census	Family Record Centre, 1 Myddelton Street, London, EC1R 1UW	Tel: 020 8392 5300 Fax: 020 8392 5307
Vital Records (Scotland)	General Registry Office for Scotland, New Register House, Edinburgh, EH1 3YT	Tel: 0131 314 4446 Fax: 0131 314 4400 E-Mail: nrh.gros@gtnet.gov.uk
Heraldry	Institute of Heraldic and Genealogical Studies, Northgate, Canterbury, CT1 1BA	Tel: 01227 768664 Fax: 01227 765617 E-Mail: ihgs@ihgs.ac.uk
Electoral Registers. School Admission Lists	London Metropolitan Archives, 40 Northampton Road, London, EC1R OHB	Tel: 020 7332 3820 Fax: 020 7833 9136 E-Mail: lma@ms.corpoflondon.gov.uk
Vital Records (Northern Ireland)	Northern Ireland Registrar General, Oxford House, 49-55 Chichester Street, Belfast, BT1 4HL	Tel: 028 9025 2021
Wills and Administration	Principal Registry of the Family Division, 42-49 High Holborn, London, W1V 6NP	Tel: 020 7936 6000
Naturalization records. Shipping Records	Public Record Office, Ruskin Avenue, Kew, Surrey, TW9 4DU	Tel: 020 8876 3444 Fax: 020 8878 8905
Masonic Records	The United Grand Lodge of England, Freemasons' Hall, Great Queen Street, London, WC2B 5AZ	Tel: 020 7831 9811

LIBRARIES

Resource	Address	Telephone/Fax/E-mail
Bodleian Library	University of Oxford, Broad Street, Oxford, OX1 3BG	Tel: 01865 277000 Fax: 01865 277182 E-Mail: enquiries@oxst.demon.co.uk
The British Library	96 Euston Road, London, NW1 2DB	Tel: 020 7412 7332 Fax: 020 7412 7268
The British Library Newspaper Library	Colindale Avenue, London, NW9 5HE	Tel: 020 7412 7353 Fax: 020 7412 7379
Guildhall	Aldermanbury, London, EC2P 2EJ	Tel: 020 7332 1868 Fax: 020 7600 3384
Hartley Library	University of Southampton, Highfield, Southampton, SO17 1BJ	Tel: 023 8059 2180 Fax: 023 8059 5451 E-Mail: library@soton.ac.uk
Huguenot Library	University College, Gower Street, London, WC1E 6BT	Tel: 020 7380 7094 E-mail: s.massil@ucl.ac.uk (by appointment only)
Leopold Muller Library	Yarnton Manor, Yarnton, Oxfordshire, OX5 1PY	Tel: 01865 375079 (by appointment only)
London School of Jewish Studies Library	Jews' College Library, Schaller House, 44a Albert Road, London, NW4 2SJ	Tel: 020 8203 6427 Fax: 020 8203 6420 E-Mail: enquiries@lsjs.ac.uk
Mitchell Library	North Street, Glasgow, G3 7DN	Tel: 0141 287 2999 Fax: 0141 287 2815
National Library of Ireland	2 Kildare Street, Dublin, 2	Tel: +353 16030200 Fax: +353 16766690
National Library of Scotland	George IV Bridge, Edinburgh, EH1 1EW	Tel: 0131 226 4531 Fax: 0131 622 4803
National Library of Wales	Aberystwyth, Ceredigion, SY23 3U	Tel: 01970 632811 Fax: 01970 632852 E-Mail: unedadcyf@llgc.org.uk
Wiener Library	4 Devonshire Street, London, W1N 2BH	Tel: 020 7636 7247 Fax: 020 7436 6428 E-Mail: lib@wl.u-net.com

ARCHIVES

Resource	Address	Telephone/Fax/E-mail
Hackney Archives	43 De Beauvoir Road, London, N1 5SQ	Tel: 020 7241 2886
London Metropolitan Archives	See page 99	
Scottish Jewish Archive Centre	Garnethill Synagogue, 127 Hill Street, Glasgow, G3 6UB	Tel: 0141 332 4911 (by appointment only)
City of Westminster Archives	10 St. Ann's Street, London, SW1P 2XR	Tel: 020 7641 2180 Fax: 020 7641 2179

OTHER RESOURCES

Resource	Address	Telephone/Fax/E-mail
The Jewish Genealogical Society of Great Britain	Membership Secretary, PO Box 27061, LONDON, N2 OGT	E-Mail: jgsgb@ort.org Web-site: www.jgsgb.ort.org
Jewish Historical Society of England	33 Seymour Place, London, W1H 6AT	Tel/Fax: 020 7723 5852
Mormon Family History Centre	Hyde Park FHC, Church of Jesus Christ of the Latter Day Saints, 64-68 Exhibition Road, South Kensington, London, SW7 2PA	Tel: 020 7589 8561 *Family History Support Office - opening hours for all Centres:* Tel: 0121 384 2028
Royal Geographical Society	Map Room, Kensington Gore, London, SW7 2AR	Tel: 020 7591 3040 Fax: 020 7591 3001 E-Mail: library@rgs.org
Society of Genealogists	14 Charterhouse Buildings, Goswell Road, London, EC1M 7BA	Tel: 020 7251 8799 Fax: 020 7250 1800 E-Mail: info@sog.org.uk
Spanish and Portuguese Jews' Congregation	2 Ashworth Road, Maida Vale, London, W9 1JY.	Tel: 020 7289 2573 Fax: 020 7289 2709

MUSEUMS

Resource	Address	Telephone/Fax/E-mail
Association of Jewish Ex-Servicemen and Women (AJEX) Military Museum	AJEX House, East Bank, Stamford Hill, London, N16 5RT	Tel: 020 8800 2844 E-Mail: ajexuk@talk21.com
Imperial War Museum (Holocaust Exhibition)	Lambeth Road, London, SE1 6HZ	Tel: 020 7416 5342 Fax: 020 7416 5374
The Jewish Museum	Raymond Burton House, 129-131 Albert Street, London, NW1 7NB	Tel: 020 7284 1997 Fax: 020 7267 9008
London Museum of Jewish Life	The Sternberg Centre, 80 East End Road, London, N3 2SY	Tel: 020 8346 2288 and 020 8349 1143
Manchester Jewish Museum	190 Cheetham Hill Road, Manchester, M8 8LW	Tel: 0161 834 9879 Fax: 0161 834 9801
Museum of London	150 London Wall, London, EC2Y 5HN	Tel: 020 7600 3699 Fax: 020 7600 1058

WEB-SITES

The following are just a few of the hundreds of web-sites which are available on the Internet.

The four web-sites indicated below with an asterisk (*) contain links to lots of other useful web-sites:

NAME	WEB-SITE
All Lithuanian Database	http://www.jewishgen.org/litvak/all.htm
Archives in Austria	http://www.oesta.gv.at/deudiv/arch_oe.htm
*Archives in Germany	http://www.my.bawue.de/~hanacek/info/earchive.htm
Austrian JewishNet	http://www.jewishnet.at
Avotaynu	http://www.avotaynu.com/
Bernard Susser Archive	http://www.eclipse.co.uk/exeshul/susser/
Cemeteries in Europe	http://www.totentanz.de/europe.htm
*Cyndi's List	http://www.CyndisList.com
Commonwealth War Grave Commission	http://www.cwgc.org
Federation of Eastern European Family History Societies	http://www.feefhs.org
Images and articles on the East End of London	http://www.davidric.dircon.co.uk/illustrations.html
*Jewishgen	http://www.jewishgen.org
*Jewish Genealogical Society of Great Britain (JGSGB)	http://www.jgsgb.ort.org
Latvia Special Interest Group (SIG)	http://www.jewishgen.org/latvia
LDS Mormons	http://www.familysearch.org
Tracing your ancestors in Vienna	http://www.magwien.gv.at/ma08/ancestors.htm
Translations Page	http://www.babelfish.altavista.com
United Synagogue (HQ) (For cemetery maps)	http://www.unitedsynagogue.org.uk http://www.unitedsynagogue.org.uk/burial.html

Although the Internet provides access to a wealth of information it is important not to let it become your only interface with the world of genealogy. As I have said in the foreword - you will miss out on much of the enjoyment of tracing your family history if you (are unable to) do not also visit libraries, archives, examine original documents, and talk to relatives.

Additional help with your family history (including many more web-sites and useful addresses), may be found in the following three Jewish Ancestor publications, published by The Jewish Genealogical Society of Great Britain:

'A Beginner's Guide to Jewish Genealogy in Great Britain'
ISBN: 0-9537669-3-4
'A Guide to Jewish Genealogy in Germany and Austria'
ISBN: 0-9537669-1-8
'A Guide to Jewish Genealogy in Latvia and Estonia'
ISBN: 0-9537669-2-6

Available from The Jewish Genealogical Society of Great Britain (address on page 101), price UK £4.50/OVERSEAS US$10/£6.00 (payment required with orders please).

GLOSSARY

Bar-Mitzvah
Son of the Commandments. Following a boy's 13th birthday, he is called up in the Synagogue to read a portion of the Law

Bat-Mitzvah
Usually girls have a Bat-Mitzvah at around 12 years of age

B'rit Milah
Circumcision

Chatan Bereshit
Bridegroom of the Beginning (Simchat Torah)

Chatan Torah
Bridegroom of the Law (Simchat Torah)

Cohen (Cohanim)
Priest (plural)

Haftarah
Conclusion. The portion selected from the book of Prophets and read after the Reading of the Law

Ketubah
Marriage Contract

Kiddush
Sanctification with wine

Levi (Levites)
Assistant to the Priests (plural)

Maftir

Concluding. The last portion of the Sidrah (see below)

Mohel

Person authorised to perform a circumcision

Siddur

Prayer Book

Sidrah

The portion of the Law read every Sabbath morning in the Synagogue

Simchat Torah

Rejoicing of the Law - 9th day of Tabernacles

Stone Setting

Consecration of a grave stone

Torah

5 Books of Moses - Pentateuch

Yarmulka

Skull cap

Yisroel

Members of the Jewish faith other than Cohen or Levi

ABBREVIATIONS

AJEX
Association of Jewish Ex-Service Men and Women

BT
British Telecom

CWGC
Commonwealth War Grave Commission

FFHS
Federation of Family History Societies

FHC
Family History Centre

FHS
Family History Society

FRC
Family Record Centre

GRO
General Registry Office

JFS
Jews' Free School

JGSGB
Jewish Genealogical Society of Great Britain

JHSE
Jewish Historical Society of England

LDS

Latter Day Saints (Mormons)

LMA

London Metropolitan Archives

PRO

Public Record Office

RGS

Royal Geographical Society

SOG

Society of Genealogists

INDEX